Mondays child is fair of face

Tuesdays child is full of grace

Wednesdays child is full of woe

Thursdays child has far to go

Fridays child is loving and giving

Saturdays child works hard for her living

But the child that is born on the Sabboth day

Is bonny and blithe and good and gay.

E.Bray,1838

From 'Traditions of Devonshire'

Journal
Of A

Wednesday Child

*

By Veronica H. Ayres

Order this book online at www.trafford.com
or email orders@trafford.com

Most Trafford titles are also available at major online book retailers.

Printed in the United States of America.

ISBN: 978-1-4269-9247-6 (sc)
ISBN: 978-1-4269-9248-3 (e)

Trafford rev. 08/25/2011

www.trafford.com

North America & international
toll-free: 1 888 232 4444 (USA & Canada)
phone: 250 383 6864 ♦ fax: 812 355 4082

PREFACE

This is a three part saga; the story of Veronica Murray Ayres, an English woman whose life began in the pre-WWII days in Wimbledon, a suburb of London.

PART ONE follows her early years as the youngest of six children, leading to the start of WWII when she was evacuated from her family at the age of ten with her Catholic elementary school to a remote area in Southern England, to a cottage without electricity in the care of a former professional nanny. Later, her years in London during the war and afterwards working as a secretary in Victoria St, the engineering hub of the city while attending college in the evening to obtain a Social Work diploma. This in turn led to her opportunity to travel in Australia and New Zealand.

PART TWO, entitled 'Taking the Plunge Down Under,' describes some years spent in Australia and New Zealand, working and traveling, in particular describing the people she met during the this time and the incredible events that lead her to…

PART THREE, entitled 'The New World.' Here she meets her husband, working and living in various parts of America. Her travels often involved extensive train journeys, once again giving her the opportunity to meet people and learn about their lifestyles.

Her interest in and service to people have motivated her throughout her life.

Veronica now resides in Washington State with her husband of 40 years. She is still very involved with helping people. Her hope is that people, young and old, who read her work, will be inspired to venture forth, even 'on a shoe string,' to see how other people in this wonderful world live, and by this experience obtain a better understanding through communication with people of other nations.

ACKNOWLEGEMENTS

My sincere thanks to Leah Blair, a young university student at home for the summer who retyped my work as I can no longer see.

Also, my thanks to Jean Edwards, who helped me collate my story.

To Debi Talboy, a college student.

To my dear husband Art, whose patience allowed me to finish this project.

Lastly but mainly, to Our Heavenly Father and Our Blessed Lady, who nudged me through all my life and led me to recall so much.

CONTENTS

FORWARD

Having been brought up as the youngest of six children in a deeply religious family, looking back I realize my early years were influenced by advice from everyone: my strict father who only had to give a certain look, my mother who would wear the 'I'm so disappointed in you' look; it was enough. My four brothers kept me aware that I was young and couldn't have anything worthwhile to say. I therefore became in my early twenties someone who had to ask advice for everything.

My parents died within a short time of each other and the boys and my sister married. Suddenly, I was working in London in a good job, had a house which I shared with a girlfriend, and I had to make decisions.

I had the opportunity to go to work in Australia for two years, doing similar social work to that which I had done in London. I prayed about it, as I had prayed with normality all my earlier life. Now I needed guidance in a big way. My family did not like the idea of my leaving England. I often heard "You'll never come back." My little seven year old nephew said "I will miss you." That hurt, but I trusted in God and became courageous.

I had a place to stay in Melbourne with good Catholic friends from my school days. Then I found my own apartment near the church; that was always my first thought. Even working in London, I was able to get to lunchtime Mass frequently. There are so many churches in the city.

My second year in Australia I worked in Sydney. Finding a job right for me took a few weeks but I had prayed about it and trusted God. I joined a social club at the church I went to, as I knew no one when I first arrived in Sydney. Immediately I was involved in parish life. I met a perfectly charming, single, English ex-pat whom I thought would marry me, but he stayed a bachelor and I went on to New Zealand. I was originally meant to stay for two weeks, but stayed several months because short term jobs kept coming up, which suited me just fine as I travelled all over that great country. Each step I prayed for guidance, knowing that as God looked after the sparrows He surely would take care of me.

I learned years before then that one should pray about a situation then leave the rest to God; it works well. On leaving New Zealand my plane had a stopover in Hawaii. The passengers were told that we would have to remain twenty-four hours, as there was a failing and the plane could not go on. My next stop was in San Francisco and the people I was with convinced me to stay there for awhile, even though I was very late getting on home. Again, I was of two minds what to do. Then one couple I had flown with offered me a job in a large company, so I stayed. I met my husband. This is our 40th year of marriage.

The decision of marrying a non-Catholic foreigner was a very serious one in my mind, but the fact he was a good Christian with a super family convinced me it was the right thing to do.

My husband and I tried living in England in my house, but he could not find a job which would give him the same income or status as the United States, so we returned there. After much prayer on my part the family gave me their blessing having met Art. It was easier to go home to visit from the U.S. than to go from England each year or two to the U.S..

I now live in a small community in Port Angeles with a great church family. My husband became Catholic 25 years ago. We are both involved in our church activities and hopefully help those in need and our pastor.

My thought for young people has always been take courage, pray about what you do, then get on with your daily chores and the answer will come. Go ahead and have faith the He will watch over you; it works. He says, "I will be with you always." Why not trust Him?

PART ONE

*

THE OLD WORLD

WIMBLEDON MARCH 13, 1929

"Ronnie, bring that baby back here at once," Aunt Maggie demanded in a tone of authority. Ronnie had scooped his day old sister Veronica from her crib and proudly carried her down to the garden to show the neighbor lady over the back fence, cooing to her as he went.

I was a full-term baby with golden hair, a pink complexion and wearing my first diaper, so I've been told. Our mom was upstairs in bed recovering.

There were six of us children- four boys and two girls. Bernard, who was fourteen when I arrived, was deemed old enough to be my godfather, but Ronnie aged twelve was always my special brother; it was he who gave me two pence pocket money every week once he started earning his living.

Next came Hughie, the brainy one, fair hair with green eyes, always inventing gadgets. He built crystal radio sets. It was he who set up a 'Walkie Talkie' to each of our bedrooms. He was fascinated with electricity. Our dad and Hughie set up a bell system over each of our beds. In the morning dad just pushed the appropriate bell, from his bed, demanding a shouted response from the recipient whose turn it was to serve Mass, get breakfast started, go to early sports practice, etc.

My only sister Mary was eight when I was born. Like the two eldest boys, she had dark brown hair, with our mother's eyes. Already my mother's 'helper,' she delighted in the newborn baby. With pride I was pushed around in my pram around the block to the shops, accompanying my mother who bought food each day, stacking it beside me in the pram.

Lastly, there was Ken, five years old by the time I arrived; a beautiful pink-cheeked boy, with corn colored hair. He looked angelic. Ken kept me well in my place with, "You just be quiet!" in a scathing voice (implying, 'You're only the baby'). However, Mom told me, much later, he used to rock me to sleep in my cradle up in my parents' bedroom, singing in a high soprano voice, "Sweet and Lovely, Sweeter than the Roses in May…," that lovely old song.

All of us were born in our parents' bed, the brass bedstead shuddering under the pulls of our mother's labor. At the crucial hour the children were sent to Grandma's house, nearby.

Auntie Theresa, Mom's sister, a midwife, was always in attendance, saving the expense of a doctor. The kindest person you could ever meet. When she sat down, her voluminous lap was a warm safe haven for any child. Knitting needles clicked constantly when she visited, making endless sweaters for which she would measure each one of us in turn. She never married. It was secretly agreed upon in our house that she never stopped talking long enough for anyone to propose. Her graying hair was frizzy, but kept under tight control by a large navy blue felt hat kept on at all times. Her constant exuberant joy for life was infectious. She must have been employed by an agency that sent her on various nursing cases, which she would relate to our mom in loud whispers, when she thought we were not listening.

On her day off she would arrive at our house carrying a loaded basket. She smelled of pastry cooking and talcum powder. Kisses and hugs being spread over everyone, even the big boys who weren't too keen on her smothering affection; her coat was safely hung up in the hall. Back in the kitchen we would gaze expectantly, eyes on the basket, mouths watering, waiting for the moment when, carefully unloaded, a cream cake or freshly-baked cookies were set out for tea. There would certainly be a gift if it was someone's birthday. She always came on birthdays. If it were a school day, we would hurry home to see Auntie Theresa.

Auntie Maggie, however, my father's unmarried younger sister, was a tall, professionally elegant lady with straight dark brown hair pulled back severely in a bun. A professor at London University, she was one of the few women teaching science and doing medical research at that time. Her particular interest was calcium, in the soil and the drinking water; produce grown in chalky soil, the effects of this on teeth and bones. However, when the need arose, such as at my birth, she would take time off from her busy schedule to supervise our household in no uncertain manner. Her laboratory approach, both to food preparation and our cleanliness, made us regard her with awe and timidity.

The two women were totally different in character, not always in agreement, but always with our best interests at heart. Whereas Auntie Theresa seemed a little afraid of our dad, Auntie Margret would argue with him about what was the right procedure to take in any circumstance. We learned to keep quiet.

Our father, Edward William Murray, Ted to his peers, was an engineer with the Home Office in London, later Chief Factory Inspector. His last position, which he held for many years, was the Curator of the Health and Industrial Museum on Horseferry Road, Victoria, London. We were afraid of him, a man of few words, just like his Victorian father before him. If we misbehaved his favorite expression was "You Ninny, you!" Then we knew there was a reprimand coming, although I don't recall him ever laying a hand on any of us. He would slowly take off his belt or his leather slipper and we would cringe, anticipating a thrashing. That was enough. "Go up to bed," he would splutter whatever time of the day it was. Later someone would be sent up to bring us down, we would apologize and all would be forgiven. He was never rough or brutal, yet he demanded respect. We complied. Our friends were more skeptical of 'Mr. Murray' and kept out of his way as much as possible.

In his many business trips abroad to inspect factories in France, Holland, Belgium, Italy, Germany, even India, he would bring Mary and I back a pretty pinafore or dress- there would be fancy socks or braces for the boys. He and Auntie Maggie talked in a language with scientific overflows. Even our mom seemed a little scared of him. She was such a placid lady, never said a bad thing about anyone. Her look of disappointment, when someone let her down or did something wrong, was enough to dissolve us into tears. When things began to get too difficult for her, she would say to us, "Trust in God, He knows best." Her great faith sustained her throughout her life.

Veronica, 6 months old

EARLY DAYS

I was born on a Wednesday but was never told this- you see, one of the nursery rhymes of the time ran:

'Monday's Child is loving and giving,

Tuesday's Child works hard for her living,

Wednesday's Child is full of woe,

Thursday's Child has far to go...'

Whatever that 'woe' meant- it wasn't to be envied, so I was never told what day I arrived.

My mother wanted to call me Veronica, but my paternal grandfather, who ruled over our whole family with Victorian discipline, informed her, "You will call the child Hilda." Photographs of this man revealed him to be fearsome-looking with a goatee and gold-rimmed spectacles. My timid mother would not have dared to disregard his wishes. He was a City Councilman in Wimbledon for many years, but died when I was a baby.

I was told years later he wanted me named in memory of his youngest daughter who at the age of twenty-one, had recently suffered a heart attack, falling down the stairs in their home and later died. My parents compromised- I was given both names.

17th March. My first Sunday- I was christened. In those days you were baptized on the first available Sunday- St. Patrick's Day. I was four days old. All the family processed down the road, pushing me in my pram to St. Winifred's Church. They were dressed in their Sunday best, and I wore the traditional long robe dripping with lace that my mother had made for brother Bernard years before. Everyone was there except for Mom, who was still recovering from my birth.

Traditionally in England, mothers spent two weeks in bed after childbirth. My mother used to laugh and say, "It's the rest I look forward to."

Father Felix Rankin, a Jesuit and our long-time Pastor, was the tallest man in Wimbledon. He rode an enormous bicycle all over town wearing a long black coat with a Homberg hat. Everyone knew him. Fr. Rankin was well respected, being noted for his kindness to the poor and his great storytelling with a tremendous sense of humor. He had baptized the other children in our family. He was there to welcome me, the newest Murray, into his flock.

The family was very involved with the church. Our lifestyle revolved around its ceremonies. The three older boys served Mass regularly.

When my mother was completely recovered from my birth, she took me down herself to the church. There, with Fr. Rankin at her side, she placed me on the altar of Our Lady and dedicated me to

Christ's mother. From then on, until I was seven years of age, I wore only blue and white.

On Sundays we went to church twice, at eight o'clock in the morning, always sitting in the fourth pew on the right-hand side in our 'Sunday best' clothes, having bathed the night before. In the evening we were back for Benediction, which was often preceded by an outdoor procession on feast days. The Guilds of our church carried their banners, walking behind the girls dressed in white, wearing veils, boys wearing white shirts and dark trousers. We would process around the whole block. A magnificent affair- people would come out of their houses to watch. Crowds gathered on the sidewalk. These were big events on our church calendar.

Fr. Rankin used every opportunity to tell us about our church's patron, St. Winifred. "She was a young wealthy princess," he would tell us in his Irish tone. "She lived in the eighth century. At an early age she vowed to give her life to God. Her parents agreed to let her go to live in a convent in Holywell, North Wales. However," his voice would become filled with intrigue, "A Chieftain from a nearby town fell in love with her. When she would not give in to his wicked sexual advances he took his sword and beheaded the poor girl there on a hilltop." A pregnant silence followed the gasps of horror.

"As her head rolled down the hill, three springs of clear water sprang up- they are there to this very day in Holywell, North Wales, and did you know," he would conclude, "those stones have blood stains on them still. Many miracles have been recorded of people bathing in those springs a being healed of their illness. It is a place of pilgrimage to this day." We would sit spellbound, digesting this wonderful story.

This holy, ardent, humorous priest left a great and lasting impression on us all.

THE 1930'S

My father created in our long suburban garden a kind of gymnasium, with scaffolding poles, pipes, and swings from the two large pear trees. All the year we played out there. We grew up healthy, happy, but more especially in our own garden, where our friends came to play with us. Mother always knew where we were. Smart parents. There were no serious accidents that I remember, though we egged each other on to more and more daring adventures. If we climbed to the top of the trees we could see the Crystal Palace, near Croydon. We would sit and watch the light glinting on the colorful glass.

"Lunch is ready, come along in and wash your hands," Mother would call out to us. From high up in the pear trees, we would scramble down to run indoors and eat.

We were well aware of the importance of safety. There were no loose wires in our house. Dad did all the repairs and upgrades. The boys were his helpers, whether or not they wanted to be. They all became terrific handymen.

My earliest memory was of having breakfast sitting in my highchair with Dad beside me, when the ceiling suddenly fell on us. I never knew why. None of us were hurt, but Dad scooped me up in a jiffy and got me out of the mess of dust and debris over the remains of breakfast.

WINTER 1932

At three years of age I recollect being dressed by my brothers in a blue winter suit of leggings, coat and matching hat, then being taken out, sometimes on the train or bus, to get a special electrical or bicycle part for a project of theirs. They were very proud of their little sister. I felt very grown up and special on those occasions.

The boys weren't always so nice. A crafty device was set up to make sure I remained upstairs in bed after I was taken there to sleep.

A long hall mirror placed at a slight angle connected with the one in the landing upstairs, and that with the one in my parents' bedroom facing my cot. My obsession was to climb out of bed and to open all the drawers in my parents' dresser to examine the contents. I loved to dress up in everything: jewelry, clothes, cosmetics, even Dad's ties. However quiet I tried to be it seemed someone downstairs would call out, "Get back in bed this minute!" I would scramble back into bed, pretending to be asleep. I could not fathom how they knew I was out of bed. It was years later when we were moving out of that home that I learned about the mirrors.

AUTUMN 1934

At five years I started school. It was a red brick building, painted dark green and white inside. It took about five minutes to walk there from our house. I wore a checkerboard blue and white dress. I don't recall my emotions that first day. I do, however, recall my classroom. It had high windows, too high to look out of, and a high mantle painted dark green above the coal stove. On the mantle there was a fish tank with a newt in it.

On my first day, as I watched it swimming about, the newt jumped out of the tank, missed the hot stove, landing in front of my desk. It was chased around the floor by our teacher, Miss Edis. She was always an old lady in my young eyes, with a tall straight back. Her fair hair was pushed back into a neat ball. Her face flushed, she dropped the poor newt back into its lofty bowl and continued the lesson, her hair a little disheveled, passing off the incident with a chuckle.

During my entire schooldays I had to sit in the front row of the class. I was nearsighted, so I wore glasses from five or six years of age.

To assist her in her work, Miss Edis would bring out large colored biblical pictures as she explained their meaning. There were enormous posters too, each with a number on it and the comparable number of rabbits, apples, etc. to help us learn to count. This dedicated teacher read wonderful stories to us of historical heroes and beautiful heroines.

Our mornings and afternoons were interrupted by a crate of small bottles of milk being pushed into the room. We were all given a bottle with a straw. When we had drunk this we went outside to play for a while. In winter this meant dressing up in our outdoor coats and boots which we had hung in our own special hook in the cloakroom. Our gloves were attached to a long tape, which was threaded through the arms of the coat, hanging out on each end. We never lost them.

Walking with my brother Ken the few blocks to St. Mary's school, we would meet up with Denys- Ken's special friend. Their class was upstairs with the seniors. These two boys were always together. Denys was one of ten children, several of whom were best friends with their counterparts in our family.

One Saturday a postcard arrived in the afternoon mail from Denys, addressed to Ken Murray, 60 Griffiths Road, saying that he could not come round to our house as planned as he had to dig a hole. It was mailed that same morning with just the street number and road, no town or county. It arrived safely. Ken still has that card.

Once, the boys forgot to take me home after school, and went off to play football. My mother was not at home that day, and I sat alone in the gloomy classroom with my teacher until it got dark. Eventually my mother came for me. I was exhausted with worry and tears of fright. That never happened again; our Dad saw to that.

CHRISTMAS AS A CHILD

It sometimes snowed at Christmas in southern England but not usually. However it was always very cold. My two maiden aunts always bought me gloves and a hood to match. Sometimes it was white fur or something equally cuddly. As we went to midnight Mass on Christmas Eve this gift came early so that I could wear my new finery that night.

My mother made most of my clothes, being helped by my sister who was a teenager when I was five. Christmas would mean a velvet dress often red but sometimes blue, with long sleeves and white collar and cuffs. Mum often made me a coat too with lining collar, cuffs, pockets, etc. Quite incredible, considering her sewing machine was an old Singer 'M' series, which I have been told was from the turn of the century. She just turned the handle.

As for presents, I never saw Father Christmas (as we called him) come into my room. However, there were presents for all of us. I know I received a large doll with soft limbs but a china face including eyes that closed. My dad was a silent man but after tea on Christmas Day he would make sure we were all assembled in the sitting room round the fire, and then he opened his wallet. Out came crisp new notes. Starting with my eldest brother he gave each of us some notes. Of course being the youngest I had the least, but it didn't matter. There was something about those crisp new notes that we loved.

SUMMER 1937

I was eight. We moved, only a few blocks, to a larger house on Montague Road, Wimbledon, with a heavy brown painted wooden gate with the word 'Sunnylawn' in brass letters on it. The house had six bedrooms upstairs and two large reception rooms downstairs. The house had the date 1848 carved in the cement above the solid oak front door. Inside there was a tiled lobby with a stained glass window of red and blue, giving a warm welcome. An etched glass door inside led to the center hallways with rooms off either side.

On one side of the house a double room contained a large billiard table, with two fireplaces. We soon learned to play a serious game of snooker or billiards. Dad was in charge here too; he always wanted to play.

The kitchen was country style; a large square, with our dining table in the middle. On one wall was a great black stove for cooking and heating the house. Hot water pipes fanned out from behind the stove to radiators in the other rooms. This was the family room, as it was always warm. We would sit around the table, chat and play games, often with friends who dropped in, until it was meal time. My mother did all the cooking. We each had duties of setting the table, clearing away and washing dishes.

Upstairs on the first landing there was an alcove with more colorful glass windows making prisms on the walls, up and down. This was my mother's sewing corner. The main bathroom was enormous. It was icy cold. We loved getting into the steamy bath but hated to get out. Above were four bedrooms, more stairs and two attic rooms with sloping ceilings. These were my favorite places to play. We had our library up there too in a walk-in closet. I loved to dust and re-arrange the books on their shelves, usually by height rather than by a more suitable method. These two attic rooms had the best lookout views, over much of London.

The long back garden was mostly lawn with old fashioned rose arches across the middle. There were fruit trees- plums, apples, greengages- loganberry and blackberry yielding what seemed to me to be endless treats. Mom made innumerable batches of jam.

Dad and his boys built a 20 x 20 ft workshop at the back of the garden. A heavy work bench sat right down in the middle. A lathe was installed. One wall was covered with shelves full of old cigarette tins, now filled with nails, screws, nuts and bolts- all suitably labeled.

A skylight with reinforced safety glass gave ample light to the building. From then on the boys and our Dad spent hours in their hideaway. A switch just inside the kitchen door activated the electricity in the workshop. This proved to be the quickest way to get a response if someone was needed indoors. One day we heard Hughie calling, "Turn the switch off!" at the top of his lungs. He told us later, "I was working on an experiment and could not let go of the wires."

Bernard, with Dad's financial help, bought our first family car when he, Bernard, went to work at the local auto showroom. It was a four-door Austin, complete with sideboards. We all eight squeezed in and went for drives on Sunday afternoons down to the sea coast or into the country nearby. It was a new toy for us all, but it was to be short-lived.

SUMMER 1939

We watched from our attic windows as the barrage balloons were raised all over London, in preparation for war. They were strung together with wires, like latticework. This was to prevent enemy aircraft from flying over the capitol. Those attic rooms became home for bombed-out friends in due course.

Veronica, age 10 in 1939 on beach near Arundel

SEPTEMBER 3, 1939 – WAR

I was taken to school on Sunday morning, at 10 a.m. with a suitcase neatly packed with my clothes. I was to be evacuated to the country. At the age of ten I was hardly aware of what had been broadcast over the radio that morning. War had been declared. All my school friends were lined up with gas masks in square khaki boxes slung over their shoulders. We were briefly examined by a doctor. He looked concerned at my legs which had many bruises. "I've just got a new bicycle. It's blue and white. The pedals hit my shins sometimes- I'm still learning to ride it." He seemed relieved.

We marched in a crocodile to the station, followed by our families. A train pulled into the station, a train which did not have a destination written on it. This was unnerving. We were excited but apprehensive and tearful as we said our 'good-byes.' Then we were off.

I was lucky; my sister was allowed to travel with me as a 'Helper.' The Helpers stayed one week getting us settled. We traveled for about two hours and eventually stopped in a wooded country area of Sussex, on the River Arun. The town was called Arundel and it had a castle which we could see from the train. This was the home of the Duke & Duchess of Norfolk. The grounds of the castle covered many acres with a lake, wooded areas, and hills. There were spotted deer, peacocks, swans, and ducks. All this was a novelty to us Londoners.

While some children were taken to live on farms, I was billeted to a Mr. and Mrs. Lynn. Their little stone cottage, No. 7 Surrey Street, was warm and cozy but had no electricity or gas. The toilet was an outhouse at the end of the garden. A chamber pot sat under each bed. The home was heated by firewood in the hearth and by the boiler in the back kitchen, lit once a week for bathing in the galvanized tub and doing the weekly washing. The cottage was one of the many supplied by the Duke to his employees. This became my new home. The Lynns had no children of their own. It felt strange to be on my own with this couple, who talked very little, with a strong country accent.

At bedtime I was given a lighted candle and proceeded through the latched door of the living-room up the stairs, where the shadows stretched on the walls at either side of me. At first I was so frightened I could not hold the candle steady and barely make it to the top.

Mr. Lynn was employed at the castle as a Woodsman. His job was to feed the huge fireplaces with four foot logs. These first had to be cut and transported from the woodlands nearby. He worked day and night shifts, alternate weeks. He spoke little and worked hard. When he came home he took his boots off, standing them by the stove like sentinels, until he needed them again. His wife had been the nanny to a well-known political family. When she married, by tradition she had to leave her position, as married women were not employed as domestic staff. Now she stayed home and kept house.

She took great care of me, never letting me out of her sight, but I do not remember this couple showing me any warmth or affection. She would come to the Park with her knitting and sit clicking away while I played after school. I was also encouraged to knit in the winter evenings, by the fire, suffering with the torment of chilblains, as my hands warmed to their task. For this I was given a gooey balm, known as 'bear fat,' to put on my hands before I went to bed. Some days we would go 'wooding,' collecting sticks and fir cones for the fire. The pine cones smelled so good as they burned. At other times we collected chestnuts to roast, or mushrooms to grill. These were all winter activities.

In spring we picked primroses and bluebells, arriving home with arms filled with color.

In summer my school friends swam in the river and caught fish with makeshift hooks on string. I was never allowed to go near the river. Pat, one of the three brothers who lived over the candy shop on the corner, fell into the river on three occasions. He ran home and sneaked into the back door and up to his room. Changing his clothes, he put the wet ones in the bottom drawer of their chest. No one said a word. A few days later his 'Auntie'- as we were told to call our hosts- saw a large damp patch of the ceiling of the candy shop. The water from his clothes had dripped out of the chest and through the ceiling. Then there was big trouble.

We friends regularly went off to school together, up a very steep hill. There was even a railing at the top to help the weary finish the climb. In winter when it was frosty and later in the snow, this hill was impassible; then we had to walk all around town to get to school.

The school was a two classroom Victorian red brick edifice. It had sixteen-foot ceilings, some old abused desks and an old upright piano which we used every day. When we assembled each morning, we said a prayer and sang a song. Then classes began. We crowded in with the local children, who had such a strong country accent we could hardly understand them the first few days. There was rivalry of course, but generally we got on well together and made new friends.

Our playground was a long sloping hill in the back. In winter, this became the toboggan run. We used old tires, boards, and trash can lids. It was fun.

Arundel Park was an endless source of discoveries for us city children. The peacocks spreading their colorful green, blue, and gold tails, the baby signet swans, born beige fur balls, closely guarded by their parents. The swans would dig down in the water with their feet until the surface became muddy, releasing grubs for the babies to feed on. There were ducks and their babies, and the funny little moorhens all enjoying the lake. The spotted deer- some had huge antlers- roamed everywhere. They were so skittish, never letting us near them however hard we tried to sneak up on them.

Life was quiet and peaceful.

My mother came to visit once a month. At first Bernard drove her down in the Austin. My father never came. Mum told me later that he would barely talk about me; he was so upset that I was away. Then fuel became scarce and the car was abandoned. Also, at that time Bernard, Ronnie and Hughie joined the military service. My mother came to visit me on the bus with all the other mothers. The busses were supplied for them, but took long hours, so our visits became short. She looked very sad. Mrs. Lynn and she whispered in the kitchen. Mom always brought cookies, books, and embroidery for me, but I wished that she would just take me home with her. Her philosophy was always "Trust in God, dear, He knows best."

I learned that my youngest brother Ken was also evacuated, but to Oxford, in quite the other direction, and Mother had to visit him too. Soon, I had three big brothers in the armed service- two in the Air Force, one in the Army- and my sister Mary had joined the Women's Land Army and was stationed on a farm in Sussex. My mother wrote to each of us every week.

There was a terrifying bomb raid on London soon after the war started. Two of my school friends who had stayed at home were killed. Then all was quiet in London.

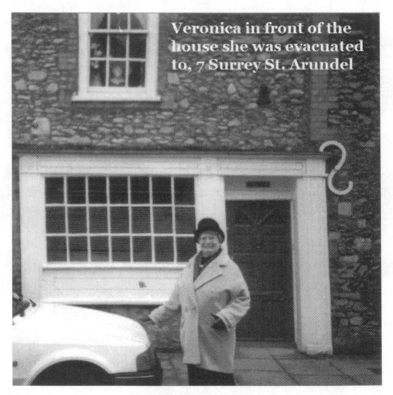

Veronica in front of the house she was evacuated to, 7 Surrey St. Arundel

SEPTEMBER 1940

It was time for me to change schools. My parents decided I should go back to Wimbledon, to be a boarder at a convent school not far from my home, but in a country area, so that I would be nearby. Air raid shelters had been built on the grounds. There was also a huge reinforced basement under the school.

My mother took me to buy my uniform: navy tunic, blazer, and sweater, white blouse, striped tie (the navy and blue being enhanced by a green stripe). I liked it. With all our packages Mom and I climbed up The Downs to school. After a short chat with the Headmistress in the parlor, my mother left. I was taken upstairs to the top floor, into a dormitory for eight. There was an alcove for a Sister to sleep; she was our Dorm Mistress. I knew no one, and the first few days were hard. The convent was enormous with beautiful grounds. We were only allowed in certain places, and those only at certain times. Some of us ventured off into 'off limit areas' hoping to see a Sister without her head-dress. "Do they have hair?" We could see their voluminous nighties put out on the clothesline to dry, but nothing else. "Do they wear undies?"

As food was rationed by then, our meals were mostly vegetables, stew or rice. Wholesome but horrible, cooked too long and in large quantities. On feast days we were given a small bar of chocolate. This we ate with our bread and margarine at breakfast. There were several day scholars who stayed for lunch. Long trestle tables were erected down the main corridor. After the meal was cleared we disassembled the tables. When day school ended we Boarders had sports. We played tennis, Rounders (a form of baseball), and in winter Netball (basketball) and Lacrosse. Then there was homework to do. Our evening meal was the best as there weren't as many of us. Someone would usually read to us during this meal. Then we had more homework or quiet reading. At 9 p.m.it was time for bed. Fifteen minutes later it was 'lights out.' All too soon we heard the dreaded "Benedictimus Dominio" sung by Sister at 6:30 a.m. as she rang the bell, and we had to answer "Deo Gratias." This was the routine Monday through Friday; Saturday and Sunday we were able to sleep in for an hour.

WINTER 1940

The Battle for Britan raged in earnest. We Boarders took to the cellars under the school, immediately when the sirens, wailing up and down with an unearthly yawn, sounded at night. We would carry our mattresses on our heads down all six flights of stairs filled with terror that we wouldn't get to the safety of the basement in time. Soon the raids became so constant that we abandoned the dormitory altogether and ate and slept under the school.

During the day the air-raid shelters were where we learned our lessons. While they were not underground, they were built of brick and were very sturdy. They had rows of desks in them.

The noise of guns fired from Wimbledon Common, only a short distance away, the explosion of bombs, and the drone of planes overhead often drowned out our teachers. We constantly worried about our homes and families living nearby. Now I wonder how we learned anything under the frightening strain of the raids. This lasted day and night for months.

There were times when there was a lull in the bombing raids. When the weather was bad, with low clouds, the chances of bombing were remote. I would then be able to go home for the day, and later for a weekend.

There was no one at home except for my parents. They had made up beds in the cellar of our house which stretched under every room, like fingers. Dad reinforced the walls with heavy beams. Home was a mess, cold and drafty. Windows boarded up, a greenhouse festooned with a grapevine but without a pane of glass. Dust and debris from the ceilings that had collapsed was everywhere. But it was home.

Spiders were my dread. When I went down into the cellar I would examine my bed carefully and the ceiling above me before settling down (there were no sprays in those days). When any of my brothers or sister Mary came home on leave, they slept downstairs too.

Our dog, Tinker, was not allowed to come down the stairs into the cellar. He slept on the top step. However, he heard, before we did, when a bomb was coming really close. At that point he decided to risk a beating and would come running down, just before the explosion.

MARCH 1941

HUGHIE, in the Royal Air Force, aged twenty-one, was reported missing and believed killed. He was a navigator on a Wellington Bomber. He was stationed in Scotland. Photographs showed him playing football and skiing when he wasn't flying sorties. The only information we were given was that a plane had been seen going down at sea, on fire. After three days the body of the pilot, in a rubber dinghy, was brought ashore. As the pilot was normally the last one to leave the plane, my mother never gave up hope that Hughie had been taken prisoner by an enemy vessel. We were all devastated. Two months before we had celebrated his twenty-first birthday. He had come home on leave from Scotland, looking so handsome in his blue uniform with the one gold wing, which navigators wore, on his chest.

MARY, my sister, eight years my senior, joined the Women's Land Army, living in a hostel- once an elegant country home- with twenty other girls. They went to work on local farms. Mary learned to thatch roofs. She and a friend, Jean, would travel round thatching the haystacks. They did not work on Saturday afternoon or Sunday so Mary would come home. The farmers usually gave the girls some produce- eggs, a rabbit, or a chicken- when the thatching was done. These she brought home on the train, hidden under her coat, fearing someone would discover her trophy and steal it.

Mary and Jean,
thatching a roof

KEN was still evacuated to a town near Oxford. He lived with a family and attended the local boys' high school. I heard little about him. He was in a quiet and safe area.

RON, my second eldest brother, went to Dunkirk with his army unit of the Royal Artillery. "There and back in twenty-four hours," he told us. His only injury: a stomach ulcer. He was made Sergeant and given an office job in Woolwich, London. He came home on weekends, often accompanied by his friends from the base. They would bring boring cheese sandwiches with them. Ron would systematically take out the cheese, make a creamy cheese sauce and toast the bread. The dish then became 'Welsh Rabbit.' In the evening he would take his friends to the 'Alex' (Alexandra), a public house nearby, known as a 'pub,' for a pint or two of beer.

BERNARD, the eldest of my family, was stationed in Southern England about fifty miles from home. In the Royal Air Force, he piloted an American Mustang fighter plane. He made Squadron Leader. Sometimes, he flew low over our house or my school, doing victory rolls after a sortie. I thought it was exciting. The Sisters would say, "Thank God- Veronica's brother Bernard is home safe again." He sometimes visited me at school and the Sisters made a huge fuss over him. Mom was terrified of Bernard's daredevil antics. After one such occasion she sent a telegram to his Air Force Station saying, "Don't ever do that again Bernard, love Mom." It was posted on the bulletin board in the Mess; he never lived that down. No one knew what he had done, but he was teased unmercifully by everyone who saw the message. He came home on leave often that summer. After a very bad air raid one night, while we all tried to sleep in the cellar, he exclaimed "I think I feel safer back at the air base!"

He became engaged to a local girl named Rose. She was a tall, attractive girl with shoulder-length dark brown hair. She lived a mile or so away with her parents. She worked as a secretary in London. Not long after their engagement was announced, Bernard was sent to India, where he remained until the end of the war. He worked under General Patton carrying out air and sea rescues in the Indian Ocean.

Rose returned to her office one evening, to work as an Air Raid Warden (all offices were required to have twenty-four hour coverage of their buildings by employees, in case of fire). When she returned home the next morning, her house had received a direct hit from a bomb. Both her parents had been killed. The whole block was demolished. Rose then moved into our attic with all the belongings she could salvage from her home. After five days, one of the salvage men clearing the bombed area shouted, "Hey, there's a dog's tail here and it's wagging!" They dug down and rescued Bernard's dog 'Musty'- named after his Mustang. Rose began looking after him. The dog was fine- he came to live with us too.

Time seemed to have no meaning, but gradually, after months of terrifying nights and stressful days, things quieted down for a while. I went home for the summer vacation. Mom was so thin and tired. Dad spent hours out in his large workshop in the garden, often asleep in a chair. I spent two weeks in the country, working on a farm, helping to get the wheat in. The harvesting machine cut the wheat and bound it into bundles, called stooks, and my job was to stand the stooks up, six in a group, to await the threshing machine. If it rained before then, the wheat would spoil.

Our house was straightened up, but then the next stage of war began: the flying bombs; planes with no pilots. They came across the English Channel from Germany and were primed to stop their engines over London. Their engines had a peculiar sound and so long as you could hear this drone, it was alright, but the instant that it went silent you dived for a doorway as the 'bomb' now fell vertically. I had a couple of near misses as I walked to school from home where I had, by this time, become a Day Girl. Once I was walking by some shops, and a plate glass window fell out right at my feet. Another time the bus I was on stopped suddenly, in order to miss what would have been a direct hit. The driver just said, "It's instinct."

Bernard, Mary, Hughie, and Ron during the war

SUMMER 1944

My father gave seminars to Safety Engineers in different parts of the country. He lectured in Oxford at Wadham College for several weeks. While the students were on vacation the engineers came for a week, using the student's quarters. By now the V-II rockets were being launched over the south of England. These were the most scary times. We didn't know in advance what was coming; there was just a tremendous explosion. Mom and I decided to go to Oxford and stay near my dad. We found rooms over a public house known as 'The Rose and Crown,' opposite the Radcliff Hospital in Oxford. We walked and enjoyed the city with its fine colleges. Each seemed to compete with the others with their beautifully manicured grounds. In the evening we would spend some time with my father. Now and then we ate dinner in the Great Hall of Wadham College with the engineers.

Without the students, Oxford was more like a country town than a university city, pleasant and unhurried. No traces of bombing here.

Was there really a war on?

Veronica, age 16
during WWII

SPRING 1945- PEACE

The family gradually got back together again. Ron and Bernard both married shortly after the war. Hughie never did come back. His name is engraved on a plaque for missing servicemen, erected beside that of the Magna Carta at Runnymede, Surry, England.

At last I left school and started to work as a junior secretary in an engineering office in Victoria Street, London. My employer had invented mobile landing strips for aircraft. The train from Wimbledon to Victoria Station got me to work in half an hour. I also attended London University part-time to obtain a diploma in Social Work, which had always been my goal. I remained in Victoria St. but changed jobs during the next few years.

One position was as a General Assistant in a small head office for a tin mine in Cornwall. The ore that was mined there was sent for assaying each week. There wasn't much for me to do, just clerical work and payroll. I read and studied for my diploma most of the day. After three years, the mine closed down; there was not enough money to commence deep mining and the surface had been mined out.

There was a marvelous view from my office window looking down on Victoria St. Whenever a dignitary from a foreign country made an official visit to London, such as the Queen of Tonga, Gandhi,

DeGalle, etc. the Royal Family would drive to meet them at Victoria Station. Each traveled in a magnificent landau, accompanied by the Horse Guards and the Household Calvary, brightly dressed astride their beautiful horses. On the return journey from the station, one of the guests would always ride with one of the Royal Family. They waved at the crowds and we, the spectators, waved and shouted.

I also had a good view of Westminster Abbey where many memorable weddings took place after the war. I would watch the Mansion House also, as the Lord Mayor of London arrived in his fine regalia for splendid functions once again, now that the war was over.

SPRING 1950

With my Social Services diploma, I now went to work in that field. My position was helping with babies for fostering or adoption; also with those young mothers who wanted to keep their babies. I visited families and made reports and recommendations. This office was close to Waterloo Station. I traveled by fast train from Wimbledon which took eleven minutes. Five minutes walk and I was at my office.

At the end of the day I would meet up with friends for dinner, attend concerts, theaters, or go dancing. I also joined the Goldsmiths Choral Society, which consisted of one hundred fifty members. This was considered one of the two finest choral groups in London. We performed concerts at the Royal Festival Hall, the Albert Hall, and even St. Paul's Cathedral, often being conducted by famous conductors like Leonard Bernstein, Josef Kripps, Ricardo Mutter, and Malcolm Sergeant. The Promenade Concerts started again at the Albert Hall. They ran every night for two months in the summer. Friends would line up for hours waiting to get into the circular area where, as there were no seats, one could promenade during the concerts. The price paid for this was a fraction of that of the seated areas.

Social life in London was back to normal and it was fun.

Something of a fluke led to an interesting event while I was in Waterloo. The Royal Eye Hospital was close to my office, and one lunchtime I called in to ask about the new contact lenses that were coming onto the market. I became a guinea pig. First, I was fitted with some large lenses covering my entire eye. A plaster-of-paris mold was made of my eyes, the lenses were produced. While they proved to be very comfortable, they had to be moistened every three hours as no oxygen penetrated the plastic. This was a disadvantage. The lenses had to be taken out, wetted, and replaced.

I went over to the hospital most days, for test on durability, etc. These large lenses became very popular for sportswear as they didn't fall out. Later I was fitted with the small lenses which I wore for forty years.

SHADOWS

Walking through St. James Park in London after work on a September evening the shadows from the trees crossed my path, like a carpet for me to walk on. Beside the lake the large gulls and ducks sat preening themselves and their friends as they prepared for the night. Smaller birds still danced in and out of the fountain as it glittered with streams of evening sunlight into the lake. People hurried by on their way home from work, aiming for the Underground. The market at the end of the park was all closed up for the night, their owners enjoying a beer in the nearby pub before heading home. Happy sounds and laughter called from inside, indicating the winding down after a busy day.

Me, I would saunter along, waiting a while before it would be time to go into my much enjoyed choir practice. We were one hundred fifty singers from all parts of London, preparing for a concert at the Albert Hall or another magnificent venue under the direction of some notable conductor and accompanied by the London Symphony or another prominent orchestra. What a treat; how fortunate I was to be part of such a glorious production!

Big Ben sounded out his Westminster chimes. Time to leave the shadows in the park, cross the road and enter Westminster Cathedral Hall, find my place among the second sopranos and prepare to be elated, singing with a host of other voices giving our best to our conductor.

1953-1956

Both my parents died within a few years of each other. Dad had cancer. I recall those tins of cigarettes, later filled with nuts and screws neatly lining the shed he built. Our mother never got over her sorrow. In moments of frustration she would say, "How could he die before me!" as if he had a choice. She joined him within three years.

Our large home was sold. I was able to buy a smaller house which I shared with two other girls, Joyce and Vera. We all worked in London and got along well together. We had dinner parties and went out to shows together. Wimbledon Theatre frequently produced plays the week before they commenced running in the West End of London- a kind of dress rehearsal. Monday night was two-for-one night. We worked hard, played tennis and tried to forget the war.

Wimbledon tennis fortnight was a feverish time too; the last week in June and the first week in July. Most evenings I would take the shuttle bus from Wimbledon Station directly to the courts after work. At that time of the year, it stayed light until 9:30 p.m. (there was no artificial lights on the courts).

Most of the exciting, fast double matches we played in the evenings. There would be about three to four hours play to watch.

During the first week all twenty-four courts were used as the playoffs progressed. Sometimes the best matches were on the 'outside' courts, not on Center Court. I followed form closely. Watching a game on Court 5 one evening in the 'garden seats,' closest to the game, I was struck by a ball hit by Ken Fletcher. It just missed my eye. He came over and was very apologetic, but to my delight the next day, was going to work with a black eye from the then-famous Ken Fletcher.

Many people who had season tickets went home after the singles matches were finished. They would either hand in their tickets at the gate, which were then given out to latecomers or, if you stood by the entrance, people would just hand you their tickets as they left- what a gift!

On finals day, as I sat home with my mother listening to the games on the radio, I said "I can't bear not being there! I miss the atmosphere, the excitement in the air. I'm going up to the courts. I'll just watch the scoreboard."

After wandering around by the Center Court stands and catching the 'oos' and 'ahs' of excitement, an elderly lady came slowly down the steps and saw me. She said, "You know my dear, my son buys me this ticket every year, but I'm just too old to sit still for long. Here you are- you go and enjoy the match." "God bless you, thank you!" I blurted out and then sat from 3:30 p.m. until 9:00 p.m. watching the finals. I could not believe my luck. Life seemed very dull when Wimbledon fortnight finished.

I needed a change, and one was about to happen.

PART TWO

*

TAKING THE PLUNGE
DOWN UNDER

MELBOURNE, AUSTRALIA
JUNE 1967

The phone rang. "It's for you!" Mary exclaimed.

"For me? Who on earth knows I'm here? There must be some mistake," I giggled.

We were sitting, Mary and I, over a cup of coffee on that first Monday in her cool green living room in Bentleigh, a new suburb thirty miles outside of Melbourne. I had just arrived from London at the weekend. Con, Mary's husband, had left for the office earlier.

They had been at school with me in Wimbledon, London. Some years later they married and moved to Norwich. Later, Con was offered a promotion in the Norwich Union where he worked. He was asked to go and work in their office in Australia for five years. It was a fine opportunity and they took the plunge. We corresponded from time to time and through their letters I realized that they certainly loved living in Australia.

In their letters they often suggested I should go over for a year or two. At first I thought their suggestion crazy, but I gradually became attuned to things Australian. I read Neville Shute's books. I made quite a study of current events out there.

One day I met a man who also wanted to go out to Australia. He was a teacher and had applied for a Churchill Scholarship. I remembered reading about the scholarships, set up after that great man died. That inspired me to try at that too.

The scholarship was for adults who had a particular skill and who would be prepared to go to Australia for two years to work. Their fare would be paid, and the necessary work connections established.

At that time I was working in London. For seven years I had been a social worker. I loved the work but the idea of helping people in a different country and hemisphere appealed to me. I applied for the scholarship.

Many months passed. Finally I was on a plane traveling thousands of miles across the world.

My friend, Joyce agreed to look after things at home. "You go and enjoy yourself; I wish I had your courage. There's a girl at work who says her friend needs a place to stay, so maybe I'll ask her over one evening. Then, if she's O.K., she could take your room for the time being. I can always call Bernard or Ron if the plumbing breaks or the stove blows up," she laughed.

My family was skeptical about my plans (I heard "You'll never come back!" more than once), and sad to see me go. Mary and two of my brothers and their families were at the airport. Tears were shed as we parted. My seven year old nephew John hugged me tight and whispered "I shall miss you."

Until then, it had been exciting but now I realized I would not see these loved ones for a long, long time. My vision blurred and I stumbled up the steps onto the plane.

Flying via Rome, where we first refueled, our next landing was at Karachi, India. We stayed onboard while fresh food, fuel and a new crew arrived. Many passengers had left the plane in Rome, and now it was possible to stretch out, put our feet up and relax. Another film, another meal, then sleep.

It seemed we flew all day over India, changing our watches to match local time. The sky was so clear we were able to view the land below us as the pilot pointed out the great Ganges River and later the Brahamputra River, weaving slowly through immense stretches of dense dark green jungle. High jagged mountains stood out clearly, stretching up from the banks of the rivers. It felt almost possible to experience that special smell of spices that is particularly Indian.

Now we were descending into Hong Kong, arriving just as the sun set over the red and yellow sails of the sampans in the harbor. The hillsides reflected a bright orange glow until suddenly it all went dark. Our pilot announced, "There will be a one hour stopover in Hong Kong."

Stepping down from the aircraft, the heat was like a wet blanket. It was difficult to breathe and almost impossible to walk after sitting so long. "Quite a shock, isn't it?" Jim had sat beside me all the way from London. He was returning to Hong Kong where he worked as an engineer.

"It's so still," I replied. "What is that strange aroma in the air?"

"Oh, that's just Hong Kong, you get used to it. Have a good time in Australia." He shook my hand and said, "Goodbye now."

We reached the air-conditioned lounge just in time. Within seconds, a wind came up and large spots of rain hit the ground increasing in intensity until it became a deafening roar. As I watched from the window the rivulets of water came together to make large puddles that quickly joined to make a river of water where our path had been. Just as suddenly it stopped raining. We were given the explanation for all this: "Monsoon time."

Qantus Airlines' hostesses took us through the terminal out to our new plane. The ground was already dry. We took off, rising steeply into a clear deep velvet sky, above the magical tiny lights of the sampans glistening on the water. I tried to imagine what it would be like living down there on a crowded boat.

Inside the half-filled cabin, comfort surrounded us: Plenty of room to stretch out and good company and food. Our new crew seemed determined that we should enjoy the ride. We were all exhausted by now and slept most of the last two stretches of the trip, Manila and Darwin. Finally, we ended our thirty hour journey in Melbourne on Friday morning. My old school friends Mary and Con were at the airport to meet me.

I picked up the phone.

"My name is Mr. Larkin, Miss Murray. I have a small export business on Flinders Street, Melbourne. I must apologize for opening a letter of yours by mistake."

"What letter?"

"The letter you sent to Carol from London. You see, we deal with London all the time. Your letter was addressed to box number 5069 and ours is 5096. I guess the mailman made a mistake and put it in with our letters."

I remembered my letter to Carol, the daughter of a family friend. She was living in an apartment in Melbourne. I had given her Mary's address and my date of arrival, telling her I would be working in Melbourne and would need to find an apartment.

"I can see from your letter which I read, Miss Murray," he continued, "that you have just arrived in this country and that you can type. It so happens that my secretary has gone to the hospital for a couple of weeks, and I wondered if you needed a job. I could sure do with some help here in the office and I'd pay you the going rate."

I could hardly believe my ears. Here I was, in my new striped silk robe, enjoying the bright sunshine as it streamed through the shades, on the first Monday morning, being offered a job. It might be weeks before I could settle into a social work position with the Australian government. There were sure to be interviews, medical exams, possibly delays involved. I explained my position to him.

"You could take time off for interviews," he replied. "My business is importing and exporting. Customers telex their requirements and I do the rest. I'd really appreciate your help, Miss Murray."

I thought quickly, momentarily suspicious. Perhaps this man is in to porn business or something worse; there were stories... He sounded like a nice man.

"All right, Mr. Larkin, give me your address and I'll ask my friend here to give me directions to your office. I'll try to be there after lunch."

When I put down the phone I realized I had never so much as been into the city of Melbourne and here I was offering to work there!

"Mary," I called, "Guess what, I have a job- starting after lunch!"

"I'm delighted for you, Veronica!" We dressed hurriedly and she drove me to the railway station.

My first purchase in Australia was a roundtrip railway ticket. The train arrived and Mary wished me luck. Benleigh to Melbourne took about thirty minutes by train, and then I took a tram, as directed, up Flinders St. to Mr. Larkin's office.

I walked in smiling, made buoyant by my success so far. "Mr. Larkin? I'm Miss Murray."

He was a sturdy individual with the leathery skin of the outdoors type. His beer belly was covered by a cowboy checkered shirt. He wore dark jeans, high boots and a black bow tie. In his thirty's, I thought.

He turned and rose to his feet, smiling. "Good on yer. Thanks for coming in so soon. You found your way OK?" I nodded. "Great, I could sure do with some help."

He took me into a back office, flooded with papers and yards of telexes over the floor. My heart stopped when I saw the electric typewriter. The unfamiliar machine looked complicated.

"Sit and practice for a bit, then we'll get to work." He left me to it. I typed- it skipped, I swore, but in a while I had mastered the machine pretty well. I smelled coffee.

"I've just made coffee, want some?"

"Yes, I could do with a cup. Thanks, Mr. Larkin."

"Hey, call me Joe." He made me feel comfortable.

The desk wasn't bad. A pot of red geraniums sat in the window. There was a nice view down Flinders Street. His girl must have things well organized when she's here. I could hear a radio playing softly. I learned how the telex machine worked, even took some telephone calls. I typed a couple of letters from Mr. Larkin's scribble. All in all, it was an interesting afternoon.

Then it was five o'clock.

"Time to go home!" Joe called from his office. "Thanks for helping. See you in the morning, about nine, O.K.?"

"All right Joe, and thanks, I've enjoyed today. See you in the morning!"

Outside it was pitch black; I had forgotten it would be. It was a beautiful deep blue velvet evening, warm and balmy. The rush hour was in full swing. I pushed my way onto a crowded tram. Someone told me, "Get your ticket first, luv, from the conductor at the bus stop." I scrambled to get off. "Got ten cents? O.K.. Here you are, jump on." The tram had waited for me.

I arrived at the station, a monumental Victorian structure in red brick with several wide entrances. I had no idea how to get to Bentleigh. So many rushing people- lines of bodies waiting before train barriers. As the trains arrived, the barriers were removed and the mass of humanity surged forward, hurrying to get to the train.

I yelled, "Bentleigh?"

"Platform Eight," a uniformed officer replied. Off I went.

Standing on the crowded train, I recognized some of the names as we made stops, but between stations it was pitch black. I could have been back in London, on the Underground.

"Bentleigh," the guard called. There was a mass exodus and I hurried to get off too. The guard saw everyone off the train, waved his flag and jumped back on the train as it left. The ticket office was closed. The platform was deserted in a minute. People got into cars and left. There were no taxis. What now? I was stuck. Looking around I found a phone booth, but there was no light inside.

"Vandals! Dammit," I swore, "they have them here too."

Taking my address book out under an old street lamp, I found Mary's number. Back at the phone booth I tried to see. The old fashioned dial went the other way around. Nine, eight, seven...

At that point I heard a voice behind me that made me jump.

"Hey, working girl, want a ride home?" It was Con; I could have hugged him. "We guessed you'd be here about now, so I thought I'd sit in the car and wait for you. I got home early today. Mary's at home getting dinner ready."

"Boy, am I glad to see you," I said. "How does this thing work, anyway?" He showed me the light switch, on the ceiling as you walked in. Who'd have thought of that.

"You dial the number, wait for the ring, then put your ten cents in the slot. It's just like England, but the dial is backwards here; we are down under, you know." We laughed. I was so relieved to see him.

I relayed my day of excitement to Con on the way home. The smell of good food greeted me as the door opened. Mary, all smiles, asked anxiously how I had got on. We discovered that Con and I could catch the same train in the morning into Melbourne. Mary drove us to the station about eight a.m. The train, when it came, was already crowded with too many bodies. Pushing our way in, I realized that everyone carried a briefcase and held a newspaper. Some were busy with the crossword puzzle, looking intently into space, searching for the right word. Others slept.

Once in Melbourne, Con and I went our separate ways and arranged to meet in the evening at the train station so we could travel back together. I took the tram like and 'old-timer,' purchasing my ticket first from the conductor on the street.

Joe waved at me as I entered the office and pointed to the coffee pot. He was already on the phone and the telex machine was spewing tape. It was as if I'd been working there for years. I took the hint and poured a cup of coffee for Joe and one for myself and got to work. The air-conditioned office made a pleasant change from the stuffy train.

Joe let me go for two interviews with the state of Victoria's Welfare Department. Their office was just up the street, across from the hospital. It was to this hospital I was sent for my medical exam. I could not get over how pleasant and easy-going everyone was.

In two weeks I had a letter telling me to report for work at the State Offices. Joe's girl was due to return to work. Everything had worked out so well. I thanked God.

Con and Mary were wonderful. We went shopping and compared prices to those in England. I bought newspapers and scanned the 'For Rent' column, looking for an apartment.

On Sunday we went into the country for a picnic. The countryside was so beautiful and woodsy. The trees were mostly eucalyptus, and their scent was heavy in the air. So many variations, shades from dark green to grey, each with leaves of individual shapes and patterns. Con remarked, "There are supposed to be over seven hundred varieties of eucalyptus trees, but I haven't counted them." He had an infectious giggle.

The large rosella birds, with their green wings, crimson breasts, and blue plumage, landed on out table, even on our shoulders, trying to steal our lunch. There were hundreds of them- and so tame! Everything fascinated me. Other families were cooking at the BBQ pits. The little children chased the birds. I began to enjoy this new lifestyle.

I had contacted Carol. She knew of an apartment close by hers where I might stay. She contacted her friend Joan who lived there. Joan and I met. She had a large two bedroom flat; I could have a bedroom and share the rest of the place. It seemed ideal, so I moved in. It was nearer to Melbourne, but I still took the train each day to my new office in Flinders Street.

As a social worker in the Victoria State Children's Department, my job was helping families with problems, habitual school delinquents in particular. To my surprise, after some orientation time, I was given a driver two days a week. The territory to be covered was over six hundred miles.

My driver, an older man, had retired from the taxi service. His leathered skin, shabby clothes and slouched gait told me he'd had a hard life, but he knew his way around. His old eyes twinkled with humor and he was not without a song on occasion was we bumped our way up and down the State of Victoria through the miles of empty countryside, with no paved roads. We carried a shovel, some rope, a water bottle and a bucket of sand in our vehicle. I realized why it was necessary to have an experienced driver.

The homes we visited were often miles apart, poorly constructed on poorer soil. Sometimes a few hamlets would be clustered together, then nothing for miles around. May task was easy: I just told the driver the address I wanted to visit, and left the potholes to him.

One of my collegues in the office, trying to be helpful, once told me, "The more dogs a family has, the more problems you'll find." He pulled his trouser leg up and showed me a nasty scar. "That was one of the Johnson's dogs," he laughed. I shuddered. "That family is in your territory. Just don't get out of the car. Honk the horn and shout. Then they tie the dogs up." I was none too happy, but it was a challenge.

I discovered that Australian children lived a much freer life than those in England. There was so much spare land and everyone had a variety of animals. Sometimes the families wanted the youngsters to help out in the farm or do errands instead of attending school. However, the problems were basically the same as in London.

At the weekends I often visited Mary and Con and met a number of new friends. Small dinner parties were the popular pastime, everyone competing to make the tastiest meals.

Food was inexpensive compared to home. The warm climate gave a wide variety of fruits and vegetables, some- like papayas and mangos- I'd never seen before.

Melbourne, I discovered, was a Victorian type city with high structures, many red brick with pale decorated facades. There were plenty of restaurants, churches, lovely large stores, a few cinemas and fewer theatres.

It was considered the thing to do to book up for the five winter ballets and operas that came to Melbourne each year months in advance, to be sure of a seat. This was the social life in winter in the city: long dresses, men in evening suits, and late dinners after the shows.

The River Yarra paved its way through the city but was almost dry when I arrived; there had been no rain for almost a year. The trees in the park through which the river ran were encircled by ditches so that the irrigation system would get to the roots. It looked awful, but was a necessity. There were flower beds still full of the brightest, largest blooms. As pretty as England, I thought.

Joan, whose apartment I shared, was compatible. She had lived and worked in Asia for years before retiring. A single woman, she loved to read, drink and eat, preferably alone and in bed. We gave some fine small dinner parties to our growing number of mutual friends. I was out most of the time. Everyone was so friendly and generous, wanting to show me their homes and their countryside. I listened to their interesting stories, told with such good humor, many about how they came to Australia.

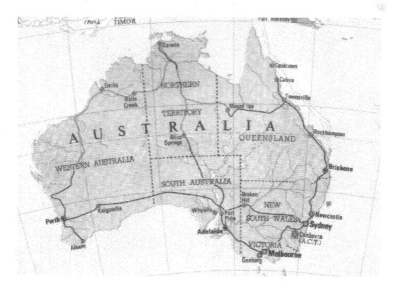

Koalas

DOROTHY

Dorothy arrived in Australia from London about the same time I did. We became acquainted. There was very little distance between our two apartments; in fact the separation was only a park with some tennis courts. Finding racquets wasn't difficult. After that we played frequently after work in the evening. By coincidence, Dorothy had taken a job in the Children's Home in Melbourne, where abandoned and needy children were taken care of. Although the home was run by the State of Victoria, our jobs had no connection. However, our employer was the same, which proved to be to our advantage later when we needed to ask for our extended time off to travel to the Outback.

Dorothy had brought her guitar from London and loved entertaining the children in the home. She taught them songs like "Puff, the Magic Dragon," which they sang heartily on trips out in their bus. Sometimes I went with the groups on picnics, to the movies, museums, etc as a helper.

Some weekends we two would load up Dorothy's little red car and just drive off to see as much of the outlying areas as we could. We discovered the unspoiled beaches as well as miles of wooded countryside. The State of Victoria covers three hundred and sixty-five miles in each direction. We often camped out or stayed at hostels.

Australia has twelve public holidays in a year involving long weekends; we made the best of them.

There were koalas and possums running wild at dusk, as well as large groups of kangaroos that would run along the side of the road, keeping pace with the car. We saw emus too, in the wild, and they often did the same thing, taking huge strides as they went.

Directly north of Melbourne is the Murray Darling River and the town of Mildurra. One time we stayed in the State Children's Reception Center there (it happened to be vacant), but we found the beds too short for us.

Dorothy had some contacts too. There was her cousin Nora at Wilson's Promontory, on the south coast about two hours drive from Melbourne. Her home was a comfortable wood-built coastal charmer, and she lived as much outdoors as in. Easy chairs and a long table made for relaxed living under the broad back patio. Faded green sun shading, complete with fringe, waved back and forth in the breeze keeping the place cool.

Nora had a son, Tony, aged about 40, who lived at home. He was a great fisherman and the owner of a 20ft rowing boat with an outboard motor. He hauled this behind his Land Rover onto the beach. He would spend hours making his own lures and sinkers.

We went fishing with Tony, using fancy lures on the end of tough string dangles over the side of the boat. It took a while to get acclimated; that boat smelled so bad. If the day was cold,

Dorothy and I would dress up in Nora's old sweaters, gloves, socks, etc. Sometimes we got lucky and caught a flathead fish, about twelve inches long, which Dorothy would cook for our supper. Nora and Tony didn't eat fish, but they sold their catch to the neighbors.

Nora played the piano. She also had a player piano in her house with piles of scrolls of the old Vaudeville music. We had sing-alongs round the piano when the neighbors came in on a Saturday night for a beer.

There was old Arthur, whom we thought had his eye on Nora. "What rubbish you talk!" laughed Nora, when we questioned her on that point. He just lived next door, half a mile away. Then there were Mary and Joe, who had known Nora since she had moved in years ago. They were good friends and knew when to go home, unlike Arthur, who would stay up all night sipping beer and telling yarns if Nora didn't use her ships bell, and call "Time gentlemen, please," when she had had enough and wanted to go to bed.

On Phillip Island, near Nora's home, there live hundreds of tiny penguins- about twelve to fifteen inches high. They nest in the sand dunes. Each morning the parents leave and go to sea and are away until sunset. All at once, they come swimming to shore, making straight for the nests, where their babies have patiently waited all day. It is truly incredible to watch their progress waddling up the beach, knowing exactly which home to go to.

Lorikeets at a picnic

WITHOUT A TRACE

Walking down a country road I glanced at the sky; pure azure blue without a trace of cloud. The trees on either side had formed into a thicket. Peer as I would I could not penetrate further than the woods either side of me. It was so quiet. I heard my footsteps as they scrunched over the sandy, pebbled, unpaved street. It was only eleven o'clock, but I was glad I had a hat on. The sun was already fierce on this March morning in Adelaide, southern Australia.

Dorothy and I had driven from Melbourne, after taking a week off of our work. Our plan was to spend a few days in Adelaide with a distant cousin of hers. As John Barret was the Headmaster of a school, we thought we would arrive on Saturday morning, when he would be at home.

The previous night we had spent in a campground in the middle of no-man's-land, where we hired an old motor home for the night. After cooking our dinner on an old gas burner, we slept on our sleeping bags on the two couches which were fixtures in the wagon. It was very hot, added to which we heard scratching as little creatures searched for crumbs from our dinner. As soon as the sun came up, we collected our things, bought some provisions from the little store on the camp site, jumped in the Mini and sped west.

When Dorothy had phoned John, he sounded excited that we were coming, adding "You'll enjoy a swim in our pool when you arrive; it's hot here."

The sign post read, 'Adelaide: 120 miles.'

"We might make it by lunch time," Dorothy shouted over the tape of Western music which we both sang along to as we sped down the long, straight, bumpy road.

Four young kangaroos ran along beside us just inside a grassy wasteland. They kept up with us for quite a while. Our speedometer read 40 mph. That's when Dorothy glanced at the gas gauge. "Gas is pretty low. We'd better stop at the next junction and fill her up," Dorothy commented. Some miles along another road sign with knives and forks decorating it said 'Georgetown: 5 miles.'

"Do you think we'll make it that far?" I asked. "Don't know, I hope so," Dorothy replied, laughing. We were enjoying ourselves and it seemed nothing could go wrong.

Suddenly she hit the brakes hard. "Whatever is that in the middle of the road?" A large heap of something black loomed ahead. As we got closer, we saw swarms of flies, then a head and legs. "Wow, it's a cow," Dorothy stated as she stopped the car. We guessed it had been hit by a big truck. The poor creature was very dead. There was nothing we could do so we veered around, almost hitting the ditch. The stench was awful.

"There must be a farm somewhere," I said. "If we see one, we should go in and tell the farmer."

We drove on for a while, but the terrain changed. Close rows of trees on either side blocked our view of farmland behind. The Mini started to splutter and then the engine died. We were out of gas. Dorothy checked under the hood. "Everything seems O.K. here. It must be the gas. I'll get the spare can out."

It was a major job to move our sleeping bags and food supplies, water cans, rope and sand bucket out, the latter three being essential, in case of a breakdown. "Here we are. Will you put that stuff back for me while I pour this in?" "Sure," I called back.

But the car wouldn't start. "I'll walk on," I suggested. "There must be a farm nearby. Georgetown was only five miles according to that last sign and we must have gone down three or four."

I must have walked about a mile when the road curved off to the right. In the distance I saw dust rising; a vehicle was coming towards me. It was an old Dodge pickup. Inside the young driver stopped and came over to me. "Got troubles, lass?" He smiled. "Can I help?"

I told him my story. "If you like, I can take you back and I'll see if I can fix the car. I happen to be a bit of a mechanic myself."

We drove back until we came to the dead cow. Then I realized with a start that the Mini had disappeared. "It's a straight road, we couldn't have missed it," I said, feeling so embarrassed. "So that's where she is!" the young man explained. "Someone told my dad one of his cows was crook. I came to see. It's Bessy, poor old dear. Now I'll have to get the knacker out to dispose of her."

"Is this your friend coming up the road in the small car?" I looked and gave a quick thank you God. Dorothy had let the car cool for a while then started the engine and it went. She could not stand the stench of the cow, so she had moved back down wind and out of the bright sun, into a shady area.

We thanked the young man for his help and he went back to his farm. We followed close behind and waved goodbye as he turned off the road.

We made it to Adelaide later that afternoon and enjoyed a scooner of beer with Cousin John who laughed at our adventures. Then we lazed in his cool pool until the sun went down.

Eight months passed very quickly. Christmas was taken up with decorating the Children's Home, getting toys for the children, any and everything to make their time a happy one. We had turkey and all the accompaniments, but this was in the form of a picnic down on the beach in the hot sun. December is midsummer Down Under.

In March, Dorothy came knocking on my door. "Look what I've found," she said excitedly. "There is a bus safari tour leaving in two weeks for a month in the 'Outback.' Wouldn't it be marvelous if we could go? Do you think we'd get the time off from work?"

We asked our bosses for leave, never dreaming they'd agree. Much to our surprise and delight, we were both given the O.K. to go.

"We Australians want people to see and enjoy all of our country," was my boss's comment.

"What a marvelous philosophy," I replied.

"There's room on the bus for two more," the agent told us when we rushed down to the travel office. We signed up, paid our deposit and started to prepare for this great adventure.

The Redline Bus Co. held two meetings to be sure we knew what we were in for. However, no meeting could ever have prepared us for what was in store.

THE OUTBACK OVERLAND
MARCH 1968

There were sixteen of us and our driver, Frank.

A Canadian couple had sailed their yacht from California to New Zealand, then flown to Melbourne to join our safari. An older man, Mr. Bennett, came over from Launceston, Tasmania. We learned he had a large farm with a hundred Jersey cattle. He traveled alone. "Bit of an enigma, isn't he? Must have pots of money," Dorothy whispered to me.

Several young people came too; four boys traveling together and a nurse from London who had been working in Alaska for a year. "I made a ton of money up there, but it was hard going; the weather is too cold for my liking. I read about this safari in a magazine. I even telephoned the agent's office from Alaska. They said there was still room, so I decided to pack my job in and come over."

"Where will you go after this?" I asked her. "Oh, I expect I'll stay in Australia and work for a while; if I can get a permit, that is."

One older lady, traveling alone, was from the east end of London and told us she was sixty-five.

"I think she saw that age a few years back." Dorothy looked concerned for the old lady.

"She's a tough old bird," Frank assured us. "She'll be O.K." Then he turned and addressed the whole group. "I've driven this old bus over our route four times now. Her chassis is strung high and we can carry all the necessary equipment for emergencies. Extra gas, water, food, sand, ropes; you name it, we've got it. You'll have a bonza time. Just keep cool. Don't panic whatever happens. If you get bitten, tell me immediately- I have remedies in the First Aid kit, knives, etc." He laughed gruffly, and then raised his bush hat to wipe his brow with a grubby red handkerchief.

"By the way, we are picking up two ambulance drivers in Queensland. They are going to collect their new ambulance in Darwin, so you'll all be O.K."

"You will be responsible for all your own food." I looked at Dorothy, her eyes opened wide. "Oh, there will be some places on the way to buy supplies. I'll let you know in advance. "

Dorothy and I decided we would diet. We bought several packets of 'Limits.' These were hard, square biscuits. After eating a couple of them, the package said, you would feel full. They needed a lot of chewing. We also stocked up with prepared dry meals, mostly made with rice considering we could get hot water in our billie cans to cook these.

Supplies included tents and ground sheets. We took sleeping bags and folding cots. "At least if we're off the ground we'll keep off the snakes, scorpions and tarantulas," I told Dorothy.

Our two boxes of food, a First Aid kit, suntan lotion, insect repellent, etc were stored under our seats. There was a small refrigerator onboard. Dorothy also brought her guitar along. We were allowed one knapsack or case for clothes. The days would be hot, but we were told it would cool off at night.

We were off on our safari adventure.

The first night it rained; a heavy, straight, pelting rain. After months of draught down in Melbourne this came as a surprise. Traveling several hundred miles north we had now left the State of Victoria and entered New South Wales. We stopped at Wagga-Wagga. Frank took us to an empty Nissan Hut outside of town. "This is the only night you'll have accommodations," he grinned. He 'found' steaks and we grilled them inside the Nissan Hut, out of the rain. "These won't keep, so we have to enjoy them now," he said. We opened some wine and everyone got acquainted. The noise of the rain on the tin roof was deafening.

It reminded me of Bernard Miles, the English comedian, who later in life owned the Mermaid Theater in London. He gave a monologue once about the Bethel church in his village in Somerset. Using the strong brogue of those parts, he relayed,

"When 'aat rains, that don't arf rattle."

Dorothy and I thought we would get a quick start and asked Frank where the showers were. "The showers are across the way. See? Down over there in that brick building." We ran off with our belongings into the shower building. I left my clothes out in the lobby and took my shower. When I came out, my clothes had disappeared!

"Is this a joke?" I yelled. No joke. Luckily, Dorothy was able to go back and get me some other clothes from my case. "This is a good start," I told Frank angrily. He was non-committal. Everyone else was warned to be careful. There was no more pilfering that night.

It was still raining when we started off next morning. The unpaved road was muddy and the terrain had become bleak. There were hardly any trees, just mile after mile of shrubs. We passed an occasional hamlet which had a 'corner store.' These stores had supplies, a bar and also served food. Everyone gathered there to get the news and gossip. We picked up provisions and went on.

Late in the afternoon the bus came to a complete halt.

"We're stuck in the mud," called out Frank from his driver's seat. We all got out and tried to push the bus. Ever tried to move a bus? I don't recommend trying for fun. Two of the boys decided to walk back to the nearest habitation to telephone for help. After a few minutes they were back. It was impossible to walk. "We're knee-deep in mud!" they wailed.

Night came early and it became pitch black. We were scared. The bus sank deeper into the mud. There was no toilet. We all agreed to commune with nature right there by the side of the bus; boys left, girls right. We climbed back in. Frank gave us a light for a while, but felt we should also save the battery. We searched for flashlights in eerie, complete darkness.

Dorothy found her guitar and started playing while I held a flashlight. Soon, we started singing. It became fun. We shared our food and drank some wine. Finally, we settled down for the night. Each of us had a double seat to lie on. It was so quiet. Once in a while there was a plop as the mud, which had crusted and dried on our legs, dropped onto the floor of the bus.

When the sun arose we were amazed to see that we were not alone out there. There were several large and small vehicles, stranded like us, spread along a half mile of road. The rain had stopped and some people had lit a hug fire further up the way. Containers of water were heated and we all had coffee. There was an air of anticipation, almost a party spirit, as we all came together to discuss the situation. As the sun came alive with heat, steam arose. The mud dried quickly.

Someone had a jeep and was able to pull the small vehicles out of the ruts. Then someone else helped us out of the deep rut we had dug ourselves into. We limped along to the nearest community about seven miles down the road. Frank knew we could get a memorable breakfast of steak and eggs, Australian style. There were, miraculously, public showers. Afterwards, we were feeling human again and were ready for our next adventure.

The ambulance crew joined us in Queensland. They were great characters. We really enjoyed the week they spent with us. Two tall, slim, fun-loving fellows with a huge sense of humor. "Our territory," one told us, "runs from Darwin down to Alice Springs. We cover thousands of miles every three months. John, here, trains and inspects new crews. He's constantly on the go. I work from

Brisbane, Queensland up to Darwin. We're in constant touch with the 'Flying Doctor Service'." We had all heard about this from Neville Shute's books.

It was hot and humid when we entered into Northern Territory, the state where Darwin is the capitol; it was the most northern town we would visit.

"This is the hottest weather these people have ever known, according to the news," Frank informed us. "It's the end of the rainy season. The rest of the year it's 80 degrees most days, and a dry heat at that."

The earth by now looked rusty red, and it got into everything. We tried not to open our cases. This meant, since we were sleeping on the open ground, we changed for dinner into pajamas and washed everything we had worn. In fact, everything seemed to take on a pink tinge at this point.

Sleeping one night in a field by a school, the air was like warm velvet- quite intoxicating. We watched the stars and constellations from our beds. I remembered that I would not see the Milky Way again, until I was back in the Northern Hemisphere.

We woke at dawn, got the billie cans going on the BBQ, ate two Limits with our coffee and prepared to go aboard the bus.

Frank provided a stool for us to step up into the bus. Someone knocked this over. Underneath was a huge deadly spider in the corner, heavily webbed in a nest. We had carried that creature all the way from Melbourne.

"Next stop: Camooweal," Frank announced. Sometime later we arrived at a crossroads and found a corner store. This was always the cause for celebration, so we prepared to meet the local people, buy supplies, have a beer and some fun.

Inside was like a party, people eating and drinking, laughing, telling the news. Two men came in. They arrived in a jeep on the front of which had a small Canadian flag. They ordered two beers apiece, then told us their story.

"We're filming for Canadian Television," one said. "Covered three thousand miles this far." The other added, "We're going home in a week though, two months is enough."

"Last night was exciting," the first man continued. "Come and see what we caught, out in the jeep." There were eight snakes, lying over the back seat. "We shot these last night in a field about twenty miles back along the road, by a school it was."

A shudder ran through me and I turned to our guide. "Was that our field, do you think Frank?" He grinned with a shrug of his shoulders. He had a twinkle in his eye.

"Mt. Isa, next stop; get your hardhats out. We'll go down the mine." Our driver was always in a wonderful mood. We went to see the enormous copper mine under the town and watched the process of mining from the start to when the molten lead was poured into block casts to be shipped 1200 miles by train out to the Queensland coast to Townsville, and thence to other countries.

"A percentage of the mining produces silver," the guide told us. "Until recently, it was shipped to England to be refined."

The town of Mt. Isa reminded me of a Western town in the movies, in the hot midday sun.

There was a library, bookstores, restaurants and bars. All had deep overhangs to shade the people from the sun. Not too many people were about, but those who were wore weathered bush hats and shuffled in sandals and shorts to the nearest shady area. The vehicles were mostly battered pickup trucks or old Holden saloon cars, rusting away.

Once again, preparing to sleep in a field that night, we noticed the elderly lady who was traveling with us bouncing around, tossing her bedding about. Dorothy went over to her and asked what the matter was.

"I've lost them," she said. "I've lost me choppers." Then, there we all were with our flashlights, hunting around for her teeth. Luckily we found them; she was so grateful she cried. We calmed her down with a little wine and once again, in the absolute quiet of the night, prepared to watch the stars until sleep came.

Darwin was a larger crossroads town; two main roads running east to west through town, one going south. They petered out after a mile or so. It was so hot and humid that we put on pounds in weight.

Our ambulance friends had left us to collect their vehicle and drive back to Queensland. We had not thought to take salt tablets with us and we drank everything and anything to keep cool. It was most uncomfortable.

At the Flying Doctor Headquarters, it was wonderful to see the trellis-work of communications covered by that enormous expanse of territory. There was always a doctor on duty. He would guide a nurse or a family member through a health catastrophe by talking to them over the radio until help could be flown in.

We went to church in Darwin. The walls were covered in airplanes, and there was a stained glass window depicting a plane. This church was dedicated to the Flying Doctor Service. We prayed for the safety of their mission.

A BBQ on the beach was a surprise for us. Frank had the boys build a fire of driftwood, then he produced some large barramundi fish which he wrapped in banana leaves and cooked. What a meal!

Some inquisitive Aborigines came to watch and soon they were dancing on the beach, accompanied by a didgeridoo. Their bodies were painted all over with white designs. When they moved together as one, crouching low, depicting a hunting scene, they were like zebras. Someone interpreted their chanting for us.

Someone explained that they live in clans or extended families, traveling around most of the year and know the best time and place for their food. They were a happy people. We sang for them; Dorothy played her guitar. Although none of us understood a word the other said, we all enjoyed the evening immensely. A very special time was had by all.

We traveled south now, passing some very pathetic settlements of Aborigines. Plenty of little children ran around with nothing on. There were camels with some of them. They offered us rides, but the poor creatures were so skinny and covered in sores that we declined. They wanted to sell us shells and straw dolls. Their smiles were their crowning glory. We gave them what we could- food and money- but we were also traveling light.

At Alice Springs we found an important city, being midway between Darwin and Adelaide. There were only a few inhabitants- mostly Aborigines. The center of town had several stores and bars, even a post office. We raided that building to send mail home. Surprisingly, there was a Museum of Art. One of the Aborigines, a man named Albert Namagira, had made a name for himself by carving and painting the most superb scenery and portraits. It was such a surprise to see this magnificent display in the middle of the desert.

On to Ayers Rock, the largest monolith in the world, which stands alone in the middle of the desert. We planned to climb to the top at dawn, as this is reputed to be the most vital time for color. However, we arrived in time for sunset and that, to me, was extraordinarily beautiful, with the pinks and purples and red shades falling on the rock as the sun set. At the base of the rock are caves that the Aboriginal people use for ceremonial purposes. There are some strange and gruesome figures painted on the walls, in blood, depicting these events.

Not too distant from there we came upon a range of beautiful mountains called the Olgas. There are twenty-eight peaks, the highest being only 1400 feet; but after so much flat land, they seemed enormous.

Our next thrill was on arriving at Coober Pede, the opal mining town. Frank explained, "Most of the buildings are underground, as the temperature varies from 140 degrees to 40 below through the year. Underground is warmer in the winter, cooler in summer."

"This is a six lane highway we are standing on, believe it or not." It was pure white in color, straight and unpaved. There were no dividers or edges.

All we could see of the town was a few small shacks, the gas station and a large cross at the side of the road. Frank said. "That's the church; it's built underground. A lot of the homes are also. You can go and see some of the homes later, they're quite comfortable. You'd be amazed how attractive they can be made. Some of them were built from old mine diggings. We will visit the opal mine tomorrow." We couldn't wait!

Around us, there were several large piles of pumice-like stones. Frank told us, "That is the discarded rock. You can go and help yourselves to the small pieces of opal encrusted in the stone."

"Frank," I asked, "Do you really mean it?" He chuckled. "Yep, if you can use a sander you can get that crust off."

"Dorothy," I called, "Look at all these brilliant pieces covered with what looks like chalk; I wonder if we could file it off."

"That's why it's out here to be thrown away," she laughed. "We can't carry much but I'm taking a fistful. Come on, let's put it in our food box- we'll make our fortunes yet!"

As at Mt Isa, the mechanism for mining was highly sophisticated and fascinating to watch. There appeared to be an endless amount of rock to be worked on. We watched, fascinated, as the brilliant colors became clear. Later in the day, we watched as a jeweler cut and formed the opals into rings, brooches, and other jewelry.

"We always paint the back black, you see, to reflect the brilliance of the stone," he informed us.

Once inside, the church looked no different from any other above ground church. Even the post office was underground.

Late in the day we visited some families who lived underground. The outside of the houses gave no indication of the delight in store inside. The warmth, brightness, and coziness amazed us. In places we could see rock, but it was dry and clean. The décor seemed to integrate the rocks as well. There were skylights, but mostly electricity was the source of light.

"Electricity is cheap here," one lady told us, "Not like in the big cities." The people were very pleasant and proud of their homes.

Adelaide was to be our next important stop. Dorothy and I would say 'goodbye' to our new friends here. Dorothy had a cousin that we were to stay with for a few days, then we planned to take the Greyhound bus back to Melbourne.

Jack lived in a modern home by the beach and was the head teacher for the high school. His wife kept house for him and their two young children, aged eight and ten years. However, before going to their house, we had one more ride with our friends in the bus.

Adelaide: a prefect Victorian city. What a change from all we had seen! How stately were the tall grey stone buildings, the wide-paved tree-lined avenues with their fancy lamps! There were Jacarandas and Coral trees, and eucalyptus groves. Away in the distance, vineyards rose up the hillside. The cathedral bells rang; it was Sunday evening.

I fell in love with Adelaide.

"Do you think we could get a transfer, Dorothy? I'd love to live here, wouldn't you?"

FOSTER'S FULHAM FARM

I visited an elderly couple from England, the Foster's, living some miles south of Melbourne. They were homesteaders and had farmed a few acres since their arrival soon after World War II

My sister in England had written to me telling me she had visited Mrs. Foster's brother in a hospital in Crawley. When he heard I was living in Melbourne he asked if I would go and see his sister, whom he had not heard from in years. I found their phone number and made arrangements to go the following Sunday.

Frankston at last! It had taken an hour on the train from Melbourne, as Mrs. Foster said it would. Now I had to find Bill, her husband, who was to meet me. I waited outside the country station but no one seemed to be looking for me. Then I saw it: a little red Datsun pick-up with homemade wooden siding. As I got close, Bill hesitatingly climbed out and we became acquainted.

He was wearing dirty coveralls and I knew he'd been in with the pigs. He brushed off the passenger seat for me and I sat down gingerly, hoping it would all wash off my nice summer dress. As we drove the ten miles to Foster's Fulham Farm, Bill told me about his wife.

I was surprised by his accent.

"Suffolk," he said. It took some getting used to; his accent was as thick as ever, even after 25 years in Australia.

"When we first arrived here we bought up three acres with an old farmhouse on it. Now the chickens are in there, you'll see. We have a new house we built a couple of years ago now, it's on the same property; our son's a contractor and he built it for us. We bought up some more land from the neighbors over the years and now we have twelve acres," he informed me proudly.

By now, we were bumping along on an unpaved road and, just as the pigs were starting to get to my stomach, Bill exclaimed, "Here's our property line. See over there- there's Daisy and Henrietta, my Holsteins. Nice looking gals, aren't they?" He chuckled. "Henrietta is in calf, she's due any day now."

We turned down a rutted narrow road and arrived at the house. I had spoken to Mrs. Foster several times on the telephone making plans for my visit; when we met in the kitchen we hugged each other, just as if we had been friends for years.

"How about a nice cup of tea," she said, smiling. The kettle steamed on the hearth. "When I lived in England, I had a home in Fulham; that's why we called it Fulham Farm." She seemed intent on sweeping the floor as she talked. I made a pot of tea.

"There is some cake in the cupboard to the right. Now, let's sit and have a nice chat."

In the cupboard I noticed sugar, flour, and my eyes widened to see Mylox for earmites, calamine lotion and bottles marked 'artificial insemination.' I said, "I'm really not too hungry, thanks."

I poured a cup for Bill. "Will he come in?" I asked.

"No," she explained, "He's gone to milk the cows, don't you hear the radio playing? He always puts it on when he's milking; says it makes them relaxed and they give more milk." We laughed together.

We sat by a black wood stove and I took in the pink paint and multi-colored linoleum floor. No carpet here. Table and four chairs, a dresser with white china. Plain wood cupboards on the opposite wall. Nothing fancy- just the essentials.

"Bill's out there milking at five am every morning- he only milks two cows now- then he goes off to work at the John Deere tractor plant in Frankston. He's worked there since we arrived here. As soon as he gets home every evening, he's out there again milking and feeding the pigs. Sometimes it's ten o'clock before he gets to bed. He's sixty-three now; gets pretty tired but he won't change it, he loves those darned animals. He won't let me touch those cows or pigs, I just get the feed ready. He says I have enough to do with the chickens, flowers and the house and all."

She settled into her chair- I saw how tired she looked. Her hair was frizzled with a perm that looked as if she's done it herself. Glancing down at the faded tweed coat she wore over her apron, she said with a smile, "This is the same coat I was wearing when I came over from England and it's still good and warm."

I told her gently about her brother and how my sister was visiting him in a hospital in Sussex. "It's like another world here- poor Joe, I hope he isn't suffering. He wasn't very brave as a lad."

Suddenly she got up from her chair. "Four-thirty already, I must go and see to the chickens before it gets dark. Come with me, I'll show you round." I picked up Bills cup of tea. As if reading my thoughts, she said "Leave it, he'll drink it cold when he comes in."

She handed me a bucket for watering and we went into the old house a few yards away. In the first room, the 'day olds' huddled round an incubator with a light in it and a moat of water surrounding it. I filled this up. Some lay very still but there must have been a hundred little beaks squeaking for food. It was hot in there, but as we progressed into the other rooms, it got cooler.

"The babies need 90 degree temperature," she explained. After each week we drop the temperature 10 degrees. This is the maternity wing." I saw broody hens sitting on their boxes clucking quietly. "These get double rations." I filled up the water bowls.

Out in the old kitchen were the laying hens, running in and out of the back door. "Here, collect the eggs for me while I clean up in here." She handed me a basket. There were plenty to gather. "When we get back to the house, mark the date on them would you dear?"

We went to find Bill, and saw two cows munching hay happily in the barn. A churn of steaming, frothing milk stood by the door. Two tabby cats were licking at the puddles on the floor. Bill said, "The skimmed milk is in that bucket, if you want to give it to the calves. I'll show you. You put your hand in the milk and gently push the calf's head down until they start to lap it up. They are several days old now, so they don't need much persuading." I had fun with that project helping three small eager mouths drink their fill of the warm brew. Finally we spread new hay for them and said 'good night.'

"Bill buys tiny calves at the market and feeds them until they are six months, then he puts them back on the market."

"Makes a nice profit, but it's time consuming," Bill added.

Over in the pig sty the noise was deafening; it was two sows with their litters. "I've never seen so many little pink bodies!" I laughed. They were wriggling and fighting for better positions on their mothers. The adults heard us coming and scrambled up. The babies fell away, then followed their anxious mothers to get their dinner.

Bill had a contract with an army service unit nearby and collected their leftovers. He separated this and boiled the edibles in a large vat, then pounded it together. This he fed into the pig troughs and hurried us out of there.

It was quite dark as we made our way back to the house. I was learning so much; it was fun too. The animals seemed to know what was expected of them.

I had noticed earlier something simmering in a pan on the wood stove, before we left to do the chores. Now Mrs. Foster took a fork and prodded about inside the large pan. Then she called over her shoulder, "Supper's ready!"

We ate a hearty stew followed by more tea. My face felt rosy, and I started to yawn. "Here, I'll show you to your room, you must be weary." Mrs. Foster led the way. I fell into a comfortable bed and slept soundly. I dreamed of having my own farm one day, somewhere.

The music from the cowshed woke me the next morning- Sunday. I guessed they had both been up for hours. I heard the swish, swish of the broom as Mrs. Foster swept the kitchen floor.

We ate a quick breakfast of cereal, then Bill drove Mrs. Foster and I into Frankston for church. He went off to get supplies.

On the way home I was able to see across the acres they farmed. "See all the flowers, dear?" Mrs. Foster asked proudly. "I send them to market along with the eggs. Those lettuces will go this week too. Oh yes, there are some one gallon pots of junipers I potted up too. Remind me Bill, when Dan comes to pick up."

I noticed the front lawn was very overgrown and offered to mow it. "All right," said Bill, "that's a job I had on my list that keeps getting put on the bottom. I'll get the mower and fill her up." A great old monster of a mower was brought out to me. It coughed and spluttered a few times but eventually settled into a loud purr. I was pushed and pulled up and down. How many horses? I wondered-more than the little one I had back home.

Every now and then as I maneuvered over an uneven mound of grass the thing popped and stopped. I had to go and find Bill to start it. "It's no golf course, is it?" he laughed. He pulled the cord a few times and off she went again. It got finished; I was hot and tired.

Back at the house I collected the eggs and filled the water bowls for the chickens. Time seemed to fly.

"Time to catch the train," called Bill. I didn't want to leave. He drove me to the station in the little red pick-up but now I hardly noticed the smell of the pigs. I wondered if that was because I smelled like them. How I longed for a shower and an early night.

Bill thanked me for coming. He held my hand and told me, "Mrs. Foster had a mild heart attack a while back. She just hasn't been the same since. She forgets- doesn't have the 'get up and go' she used to have. You will come again, won't you? I know she was happy to see you and glad of the help. She doesn't say much though." He handed me my hold-all and gave me a friendly pat.

I slept all the way back to the bustling city of Melbourne.

During the next few months I often went down to Frankston. One weekend I planted maize behind Bill's tractor. Up and down, up and down the field. We planted more vegetables too. The growing season here was a long one.

"We can get two crops in most years," Bill explained.

Every time I went into the house, it seemed Mrs. Foster was always sweeping the kitchen floor. She seemed to be leaning on the broom more than pushing it along. The calves went back to market.

"Will you get some more?" I asked. Bill didn't think so. "Mum's not doing so well these days, she's got enough to do." She never complained.

"Bill took the piglets to the market last Tuesday, borrowed old Joe-from-down-the-road's big truck. They brought in a good price. Keep us in feed for a while." She looked all-in.

"Have you been taking your medicine?" "Heavens no," she replied. "I reckon when the good Lord wants me He'll take me; no good fighting it."

I went to bed tired out but with a good feeling inside me. These days I had taken over most of Mrs. Foster's duties on the weekends. I enjoyed the change of scene from city life and felt quite at home. I really loved this couple. They seemed to like me too.

Next morning I rose early. I thought, "I'll take Mrs. Foster a cup of tea in bed." She lay there peacefully. She had drunk her last cup of tea. I couldn't believe what my mind was telling me.

Going out to the cowshed, I had to scream at Bill over the music. "Come indoors! Something's happened." He came in and assessed the situation quite calmly, sitting on the bed.

"I'll go and get our son, He'll know what to do. Will you stay with her?" The son came and they talked for a while. I did the chicken chores and cleared up in the house. "Would you like me to stay on for a day or two, Bill? I'll take a couple weeks off work if you like," I offered. "No thanks, we'll manage."

He drove me to the station as usual. "You must come down again, any weekend you feel like it. My son is going to take the small animals over to his place; his wife will take care of them." We shook hands and I hugged him. He did smell bad.

Sadly, I knew I'd spent my last weekend out at the farm. As I sat alone on the train, the tears came. I knew I would miss this country life, these lovely people. At least Mrs. Foster was at peace; poor Bill…

TASMANIAN INTERLUDE

The small plane took over an hour to fly from Melbourne south to Hobart, capitol of Tasmania. It was midwinter in the Southern Hemisphere.

I chose the early morning flight for the view, but what I didn't expect was to see the thick white frost covering the pine trees and glistening over the fields. The rivers and lakes looked as if they were frozen over; my suspicions were confirmed as I watched some ducks skate to a stop on the surface of the water.

The hills and valleys reminded me of Surrey, in England.

As the Cessna landed we flew over the natural and beautiful harbor of Hobart. Several cargo ships were being loaded from the docks. The rest of the waterway was filled with various pleasure boats, from large yachts to small fishing vessels. The place was alive with beaver-like activity despite the cold morning.

A tall blond, bronzed man approached me.

He greeted me with a boyish grin. "Good on yeh, you made it- in that little kite." His handshake was huge and warm.

"Thanks for coming to meet me, Charles. I hear you are the busiest man in town. Joan must have given you a good description of me; she certainly described you well."

A week earlier I had mentioned to my girlfriend, whose apartment I shared in Melbourne, that I would like to visit Tasmania for a few days. The long weekend for the Queen's Birthday was fast approaching, so I might be able to get a couple days off work. Joan immediately sat up excitedly. "My sister Peg lives in Hobart with her husband and two girls- I'll call her." Later, Joan rushed into the kitchen. "They would love to have you stay with them for the weekend!"

Charles took over collecting my baggage and leading me to a large pick-up truck outside the airport. The truck had a large sign saying 'Tasmanian Apples- We Deliver Anywhere.' My host explained that this was his business; he had built it up over twenty years.

"It started as a small shop delivery service during the summer vacation while I was still in high school." He pointed to the labels on the crates: LONDON, PARIS, DUBLIN. I was impressed.

"Peg and the girls are waiting at home, the kids are so excited to be meeting someone from England. They're planning all kinds of sightseeing trips for you. There's the Grand Ball tomorrow night for the Queen's birthday celebration. You'll meet most of the town there; it's a good excuse to 'gas up.' You do like beer, don't you?" His eyes twinkled; they were bright blue.

"Sure, I like beer, but I can't drink it the way you Aussies do- it's too full of gas."

We were travelling away from the city and I caught sight of a sign 'Kingston Bay 20 miles.' Charles explained, "Our home is in Kingston Bay. I travel this road every day to the warehouse. "

Turning a corner later, he pulled the pick-up to a stop on the sandy beach, about thirty feet from the ocean.

"There's never much of a tide here," he grinned, I think to reassure me. Jumping down he grabbed my hold-all, then helped me down. "Ready for a climb?"

Pulling my eyes away from the sparkling ocean, I followed him up a winding stairway that seemed to go to the sky. As we ascended, the view became more spectacular. Resting a moment, I spotted little fishing vessels bobbing on the tide. There were some surfers too, riding the waves. Birds skimmed on the surface of the water. Then I spotted a sailing dinghy nestled into a cove. "That's my pride and joy," Charles shouted back after me.

Another bend and steps led onto a balcony running the length of a white chalet-type house. Peg was there to greet us. Behind her stood two young girls.

Charles said, "Peg, this is Veronica." Then to me, "Meet Jo, our fourteen year old, and Kathy, who is eight." The girls went in to set the table while Peg and I got acquainted, sitting on the balcony. It was like being on the top of the world with a wonderful view that went on forever. In a while, Charles came with a tray of drinks. He wanted to know what his wife had planned for the weekend.

We spent a happy evening together. Peg was like her sister, but younger. She had the same golden bronzed hair, but I had never seen Joan with her hair down, it was always scooped up and twisted in a chignon. Jo and Peg had long tresses, pinned back off their healthy sun-tanned faces. Young Kathy had blond hair and obviously took after her dad. She had forgotten her shyness when we first met. Now she told me about tomorrow.

"We are going to have a picnic up on Mount Wellington. It's the highest part of Tasmania. Did you see it from the plane?" I nodded. "In the evening I'm going to sleep over at Jenny's house-she's my best friend. You're going to the Ball with Dad, Mum, and Jo's coming too. It's her first dance. You should come and see her dress!"

We all went inside. The dress was a frothy taffeta, pale green blended with gold. There were gold shoes to match. "You'll be the belle of the ball, Jo," I said. "I'm looking forward to seeing you dressed up."

Peg followed me into my room, carrying a red tartan skirt. "Would you like to wear this skirt tomorrow night with a white or black top?"

"I'd love to. I was wondering what I would wear to such an event as a ball." We laughed.

Next morning we set off in the Rambler, up the steep winding road to Mount Wellington. There was snow all around us, the air was crisp and clean, but the sun was warm. We chased about and threw snowballs. There weren't many other people about. "They are all preparing for the Ball," Charles confided in me. "You have no idea how long it takes for hair, nails, and make-up. Living with three women I've learned a lot."

Peg produced hot soup from a thermos, we enjoyed this with French bread and some cheeses. It all tasted marvelous in the fresh air.

On the way home we sang folk songs from England, Wales, and Ireland, then some traditional Australian melodies, ending with the Beatles' songs. It was great fun. The girls told me they learned the songs at school. On Empire Day, they put on a display of country dancing from different countries. It took me back to my days at school.

No sooner were we home then there was a feverish rush for showers, hair curling, and frantic rushing from room to room, just as Charles said there would be. He took Kathy over to her friend's to spend the evening; I noticed a teddy bear went too.

The Ball was a tremendous success. At first it seemed overcrowded in the hall, but gradually people drifted off to the bars or sat outside chatting with their friends. The dance floor was also very popular. Charles danced with Peg, then came back and offered his arm to his daughter, who looked stunning in her ball gown.

Drums rolled. The Toastmaster, dressed in full kilt regalia, made an announcement. "Ladies and Gentlemen, please be upstanding. Raise your glass for a toast to Her Majesty." Chairs were pushed back, and then came to roar: "Her Majesty, God bless her!"

I was introduced to everybody, it seemed. At about midnight it was all over. The 'good nights' said, everybody drifted home. I turned to my gracious hosts. "That was wonderful, thanks so very much for including me."

My second day in Tasmania was a history lesson. We drove down to the Penal Settlement at the very south of the island, over several bridges linking it to the mainland.

Charles explained to me, "It was here that the first settlers came, in chains. It was the convicts and their jailers. They had to build their own prison. What stands today is a monument to these men." We went down long, damp corridors. Some of the cells still had chains hanging from large rings on the wall. The place gave me the shivers. I was glad to get out into the warm open air and find a cricket match in progress. We sat and relaxed, watching the game, eating sandwiches. I bought cards from the little gift shop. It was sobering to think of the lives of the convicts.

Too soon it was time to return across the long bridges back to Kingston Bay. We sang some more songs, but Charles question brought us to silence. "Say, what time does your bus leave tomorrow, Veronica?" I was going to travel to the north of the island to

Launceston. A man I had met on our safari had invited me to spend time with him and his wife on their farm up there.

It was sad to part from this lovely family who had been so friendly to me. They all came down to the bus station. I waved good-bye. There was a lump in my throat. I had only known them three days, yet I know I would never forget their kindness to me.

The journey north was through the miles of orchards, mainly apples. Numerous homesteads dotted the fields along with a mixture of cows, sheep, and produce. Machinery was being used, but none of the huge combine harvesters I'd seen in Australia.

The frost was visible clinging to the trees all morning. We stopped for lunch at the town of Ross, almost at the center of Tasmania. We were taken to a country hotel where a welcoming fire blazed. Hot soup and delicious sandwiches were brought out to us. Then, back on the bus. We traveled for another four hours.

The day was now warm and sunny; the countryside brilliant green. Few settlements were visible and few people could be seen. The land had a woodsy appearance further north. Our journey ended as the light started to fade about five p.m. I had no idea the island was so beautiful or so large.

Mr. Bennett met me as planned; his wife was with him. This couple was in their sixties and they were well and warmly dressed. Their almost new Rover took us to their model rambling farmhouse.

The last time I had seen Mr. Bennett was in Adelaide, as we ended our Outback Safari. His wife seemed very interested as we recalled some of the incidents on our trip.

"I would have loved to come with John," she commented, "but as we have a farm, one of us has to stay here. I took off once John had got home."

"Where did you go?" I asked her.

"Back to Oxford, England. I still have family over there. It's always wonderful to go home, but it's also wonderful to come back to this unspoiled, peaceful heaven of ours. Isn't it, John?"

After a hearty beef dinner, some wine and good company, I was ready for bed.

In the morning light Mr. Bennett took me with him on his round of the farm. This was an intensive modern farm. Given the grand tour, I saw seventy Jersey cows as they mounted the ramp into the rotary parlor, where they were milked automatically, at elbow level, then continued out into the yard. Everything was modern equipment. The whole process finished in less than one hour.

There were pigs housed in cement runs, again with automatic watering devices and food distribution. It amused me to see their dexterity in getting food. There were no foul smells. At determined intervals the runs were sprayed down. I enjoyed my morning tour of this modern farm.

Mrs. Bennett collected semi-precious stones. She had a workshop where she enjoyed polishing the stones and making jewelry, decorative lamps and other lapidary craft work. She put on boots and a warm coat, and dressing me likewise, we went hunting on their beach in the afternoon, looking for garnets, greenstone, quartz, etc. We were not too successful as it started to rain heavily. As we returned home I asked Mrs. Bennett, "Don't you feel very isolated, living so far from neighbors and town?"

"Well, when that happens, I just tell John I'm going to Melbourne or Sydney for a week. That's enough. I come back refreshed."

I spent another cozy evening round the fire with this interesting couple, drinking home-made wine and listening to some fine classical music, and then it was time for bed.

In the morning Mr. Bennett took me to the airport and Launceston, where I caught a plane back to Melbourne.

Back in Melbourne, I thought it was time to see more of this beautiful country, and having told my friends I was going to Sydney, we had a farewell party. I left on the early train to my new destination.

SYDNEY
OCTOBER 1968

Margaret Pincus, whom I had met in Melbourne, gave me the name of a friend of hers in Sydney.

"Do call him up- you'll like him. We've known him for years. He used to spend a lot of time at my parents' house in Caulfield. He's a physicist; works in the Sydney Government Laboratory, it's called CSIRO. He's single too. His name is Tony."

"Thanks, Margaret, I'd love to get in touch with him. He sounds interesting." As I left Melbourne on the train for Sydney I contemplated how I would approach Tony.

When I plucked up the courage to call his office, I was told 'Tony is in England on leave' and 'No, we don't know when he will be back.' Disappointed, I patiently waited a week and called again, only to hear 'No, Mr. Clarke is not back yet.'

I persisted and after several weeks when I telephoned again, I heard a bright, slightly North Country accent say "Hello, this is Tony." Startled, speech left me momentarily. I then explained that Margaret Pincus had suggested I get in touch with him as I had just arrived in Sydney.

"Oh yes, I know Margaret. I've known her family for many years. Her mother was a great Scrabble player; we would stay up until the early hours playing. She passed away last year. Her father, Paul, is a brilliant scientist. Have you met him?"

"Yes, as a matter of fact he worked with my aunt at London University- researching teeth and bones, I think. He invited me to their home in Melbourne too. He makes wine from his own grapes. I enjoyed going over and visiting with him and Margaret very much."

Tony asked if I would like to have lunch with him on Sunday. "Yes, that would be great!" He must have heard the excitement in my voice.

The following Sunday at noon, carefully dressed in a green floral dress that I felt was a winner, my fair hair shining, I went to meet him.

Alighting from the bus at Rose Bay, I found this tall, well dressed Englishman, bronzed by the Australian sun. Late thirties, I guessed, with a typical light-weight sports jacket, open necked shirt, and fine grey flannels. His fair straight hair was a little unruly in the warm breeze. He wore gold-rimmed spectacles and his infectious smile put me at ease. My heart skipped a beat.

He carried a bottle of wine wrapped in black tissue paper with the words 'Blue Mountain Finest Wines' in gold lettering. "We can take wine into a restaurant here," he explained. "They don't have a permit to sell it. My father owns a wine shop in Wolverhampton. Do you know the area?"

Our conversation ran smoothly; I was fascinated by his every word. "My employer in Melbourne," I told him, "was so sure I wouldn't like it in Sydney, he refused to let me go. He told me, 'Take a leave of absence. You'll be back.'" I laughed. "But I only have one more year in this huge and wonderful country. I must see more of it."

He read over the menu. "The fish is very good here, I can recommend it."

"I love fish. I'll have whatever you suggest."

"Calamari is one of my favorites," he told me.

We talked non-stop. The view over Sydney Harbor was breathtaking. Sailing boats bobbed along, ferries carrying sightseers zig-zagged across the bay. Black swans hugged the bank, looking for scraps of food. I could see the jacaranda trees with their cascades of blue blossoms gently swaying in the noon breeze.

"I went into the army at eighteen," Tony told me as he topped up our glasses. "When I was discharged, my idea was to go to a university, but there was a waiting list for three years in England. Then I saw an advertisement in the Telegraph that Australia was offering university places in Melbourne, for ex-servicemen and women if they would emigrate.

"I decided to come over here. My father agreed it would be the best thing. He wanted me to take over his wine shop eventually when he retired but that wouldn't be for a few years. I became a physicist. Do you know what that is?" I nodded. "The job I have now is the one I took straight from Melbourne University. The laboratory is run by the Government. Great pension scheme; I'll be retiring in a few years," He chuckled. ""That's the way it is here. It's a young person's country."

"You must love your work."

"It's very exacting. We set the standards of measurement, you know. Alcohol content in whiskey, for instance. It had its compensations; we have to dispose of the contents." Again that small laugh- Not a large guffaw, but an 'I'm enjoying life' laugh. He asked about me.

"I really didn't want to leave Melbourne, I'd made such good friends there. Sydney seemed the next logical step, then perhaps Brisbane." He was so easy to talk to...

A flying boat gracefully landed on the harbor in the front of us. "That's the plane from St. George Island, off the coast here," Tony explained. We watched the passengers alight. They seemed in high spirits, prepared to enjoy a day in Sydney.

By the end of the meal I felt I had known him for years. We strolled comfortably by the bay, and then, on an impulse, jumped on a ferry boat to the north side of the harbor, walked around for a while. Then we sat and sipped a long cool Pims in the shade. We crossed back in the ferry as the shadows lengthened. Later, we caught a bus together and he walked me home.

He said, "Give me your phone number, I'll call you," and was gone.

The stars danced before my eyes.

It started to rain the next day, and rained for days. I made some inquiries about a job and proceeded, with piles of coins, to spend hours on the phone. There were some interviews, at which I arrived rather bedraggled from waiting at bus stops in the rain. The beaurocracy of the Government of South Wales was strict. They were not taking on any social workers.

I began to worry; I would have to return to Melbourne if I didn't get a job. I found a clerical job advertised, right downtown. It was with the local Engineering Union. Not exactly what I had in mind. I became a member of the Clerical union in order to get the position and jumped on board. I was issued a pale blue uniform dress with my name embroidered on it. The pay was good, I kept reminding myself. The job was boring, filling in names of new members on cards and typing endless lists. I worked the switchboard at lunchtimes.

At about that time I read an advertisement in the Sydney herald: 'Girl needs second to share two bedroom apartment. Double Bay.' I dialed the number.

Maureen invited me to come and take a look over the place. It was right by the water. A small cozy apartment on the ground floor of a large old house. The bathroom had a shower above a stool so if you wanted you could sit and shower at the same time. I tried that once only.

Across the bay was the Sydney Zoo. At night we could hear the lions roaring.

Maureen was in her late twenties, tall with long curly dark hair and dark brown eyes. She looked Irish, and told me her father was a judge in Brisbane Court. "He's the Irish side of me. My mother came from England when she was a child."

We found we had a lot in common. She too was single, away from home, and loved to play tennis. She had become a member of a social club at her church, St. Phillip's. "We have a great time. Every weekend there is something going on and I'll take you down with me if you'd like."

"The last girl that was here, Erika, left last week. She worked two jobs, I hardly ever saw her. She went home to Germany; her visa expired." Maureen made some coffee, I followed her into the kitchen. "I made these cookies for the club picnic, at the weekend. Have one."

If only she liked me, I thought, this would be so nice and convenient.

We agreed on terms. Next day I moved in.

Sydney now had a brighter side for me. It had finally stopped raining too. Trees were full of almond blossom, the jacarandas gave a colorful charm as they lined the streets. There were coral trees in bloom at the park downtown. I had never seen such a mass of crimson all against the bright blue cloudless sky. This is a gorgeous city, I thought.

Tony lived in a private hotel a little out of town; I asked him once why he didn't have a car. "Oh, well, I wasn't going to come back from England this time. I even sold my boat- didn't I tell you I had a small Cabin Cruiser? Moored her in the Hawkesbury River, just north of here." We were having dinner the following Wednesday, he had called for me on Monday.

"Why were you not going to come back? This is such a splendid place," I asked innocently.

"If you must know, I had a girlfriend here. She ran the guest house where I stayed. She led a complicated life; I can't go into it. Anyway, she jumped off the roof in May. I couldn't bear it." There was silence as I digested this information. I wanted to hold him so badly.

The waiter came at that moment with the check, and the tense moment was behind us.

My year was flying by. I took a few days off work to visit Canberra, the capitol of Australia, three hours drive inland from Sydney. Tony said I should visit the capitol of Australia, even just once. It was new, sterile looking, square blocked city housing government personnel, their aides and domestic help. I visited a Government house.

Another day I boarded a bus for an escorted tour of the city; it was flat boring, and without character. After Melbourne and its old elegant buildings, Canberra seemed so artificial.

I was glad to get back to Sydney and my new friends. Sydney, where the lights never dimmed. It certainly lacked the dignity of Melbourne, but it was a fun city, I decided. The shops stayed open all hours. Storekeepers sat outside their stores relaxing in the cool night air, chatting with their neighbors, I felt quite safe walking home, even at midnight.

I discovered Tony had many girlfriends. He ate out every night as he had no kitchen where he lived, and he never ate alone. It was shattering for me to realize I was only one of many girlfriends. Tony made no secret of his acquaintances. He had many married friends too, and sometimes he would take me to their homes for dinner parties.

Maureen took me to her social club. On the weekends we would go out as a group. I learned to play golf, steer a small boat down a river, and had fun fishing. All the necessary equipment for these activities could be hired for the day. We would take picnic baskets and share food and wine.

"Everyone here is geared to the outdoors. It's such a healthy lifestyle," Maureen told me. It seemed someone always had a party somewhere every weekend: on the beach, up the river, or car-pooling into the Blue Mountains for a day hike, ferryboat parties crossing the magnificent Sydney Harbor. It was a case of fitting in work Monday to Friday. Life was wonderful; I had never had so much fun. But my mind was on Tony.

Sydney Harbor

A DAY IN COURT

It was in Sydney that I became entangled with the law and had to appear in court. It was a terrifying experience, but looking back it was also very humorous.

It was a Friday evening after work and I had been grocery shopping. The bus I took was very crowded and I was pushed to the rear with my packages. When the bus slowed down for my stop, I tried to get past people who had as many parcels as I had, but before I could reach the door, the bus took off and rounded a corner into an area I did not know, continuing to the next stop.

As I alighted a voice behind me called, "Just a minute, young lady, Let me see your ticket." I recognized his badge; he was an Inspector for the bus company. Putting my parcels down, I handed him my crumpled ticket. "You only paid to go to the crossroads, I'll have to take your name and address."

"I could not get off the bus up there, it was too crowded." He ignored my explanation.

"Name," he demanded. "Address… Age." At this point I told him that age was a private matter for a young lady. He wrote: 'about twenty-five.'

"You'll be hearing from us." He turned and walked away. Shocked, I walked home almost in tears.

Weeks passed and one Sunday morning, answering a knock on the door of the apartment, I was confronted by two uniformed men. "Are you Miss Murray?"

"Yes."

""Please sign this subpoena. You must appear at Court No. 2 on the 20th." Shakily, I accepted the form and signed for it.

On the appointed day I took the form and was amazed to see about fifty people, all waiting to go before the magistrate. We jammed into the courtroom. One by one a name was called. A short citation was read, followed by "How do you plead?"

Every one of them replied "Guilty."

"Pay fifty dollars to the clerk on your way out."

I thought, I'm not guilty. So I said when the time came, I said "Not guilty." There was a short silence. Then the judge spoke. "The clerk will give you a time for a hearing for your case. You may being an attorney."

Some weeks later I returned to court alone, wearing my blue uniform dress. The magistrate asked, "Do you have legal representation?"

I replied, "I will represent myself, thank you."

He was the perfect example of portly Australian middle aged manhood, a David Frost type with large blue eyes, what little hair he had parted above his left ear with long strands dangling, and a bright red face.

He stated that the transit company wished to bring action against me for traveling fraudulently on the bus, and gave details. The transport representative then gave his version of what happened. He submitted ticket which he stated was the one I had bought some months earlier.

I was asked if I had any questions to put to the transport representative. "Yes, thank you," I said, showing bravado although I was shaking in my shoes.

"I hope the court is not under the impression that the report by the representative was verbatim. The inspector did not take any notes, but only took down my name and address."

"Also," I continued, "I would like to question the validity of the ticket which he claims is mine. I know my ticket was crumpled up when I gave it to the inspector. Lastly, considering the inspector questions hundreds of people every week, I doubt if any of the report submitted could be verified."

At this point, the magistrate drew himself up to his full height and blustered, "This case is dismissed. Insufficient evidence." He smiled at me.

The transport representative jumped up. "B-b-but what about the courts costs, and…?"

"What about them?" The magistrate barked. "Case closed."

I walked out into the sunshine and breathed deeply. "Thank you God, for that being over," I murmured.

Tony and I had dinner once or twice every week. He often came to our apartment, and while I cooked dinner, he would fix anything that needed mending, such as my hair dryer or the food mixer. What a gem he was.

Time flew by. At the end of the year in Sydney I made it known I was leaving to go home. I thought if Tony was interested, he'd follow me. He knew I had a house in Wimbledon which my girlfriend was looking after for me. Either way, it was time to go.

Tony and I arrived back at my apartment around eight o'clock one evening shortly after this. I opened the door, switched on the light and found thirty-five people there to give me a surprise going away party! I hadn't realized I had so many friends: from the social club, from work, neighbors, etc. What an evening it was. The weather was warm, we took wine and food they had brought outside. Everyone got acquainted. We danced. There were gifts to wish me 'bon voyage.' I was truly amazed; a year ago I hadn't even met them, now I cried as we all said 'cheerio.'

A berth had been booked for me on the *Canberra*, the largest ocean liner at that time. Next day, I boarded ship with a trunk and two suitcases, filled with mementos that I had collected during the two years I had been in Australia. My trunk and one case went into the hold, but I kept a fairly large case of clothes with me. I had plans.

Tony and Maureen came on board to see my cabin and say good-bye. Maureen planned to meet me in London the following year. She and some other friends intended to get visas and work in London for a year and planned to stay with me in Wimbledon.

It was hard to say good-bye to Tony. He had been a perfect companion and friend, but it seemed that was the way he wanted things to stay. He said he would write.

THE *CANBERRA*

Life on ship bored me. It was just too chilly to sit out on deck, although some stalwarts wrapped in blankets and furs mused away hours looking out into the endless sea. After all, it was September; we were just coming out of winter in the Southern Hemisphere. I walked all fifteen decks, played cards, went to Beatle drives, exercised, swam, danced and ate wonderful food. Still there was time to spare.

My favorite place was the Writing Room, tastefully decorated in blue and white, with masses of blue and white headed paper waiting to be used. There were comfortable desks to sit at. It was empty most of the time. I wrote several letters; there were many people to inform of my change of address. It would be impressive, I thought, for them to be written on embossed *Canberra* notepaper. They would be mailed from the ship as well.

Millie Evans, the lady who shared my cabin, came from Auckland, New Zealand. A middle-aged mother of two teenage sons, Millie was a milliner by trade. She worked from home. Her husband, a building contractor, would be meeting her when the ship docked.

Millie and I became good friends, although we didn't have much in common. She had hopes that her two boys would go on to a university. "They are both mechanically minded, they want to be engineers. Mike has an old Model A that he is restoring, but the ducks keep getting into it," she laughed. "We have chickens too, and two sheep, tethered about the field. They keep the grass down."

Mille was reluctant for me to go to London without stopping off in New Zealand. It had already crossed my mind that I could leave my luggage in the hold and take a tour of New Zealand once the *Canberra* docked in Auckland. Millie was enthusiastic to help me. "You can stay with us dear, our house is by the North Harbor of Auckland, in Birkenhead. We have two natural harbors, one north and one south."

I decided to make New Zealand part of my grand tour. I thought I would have to contact one of my brothers to collect my luggage when the *Canberra* arrived in London, and give him permission to sign papers for customs.

Exactly on schedule, early in the morning mist of the third day from leaving Sydney, the *Canberra* dropped anchor and drew up at the end of Queens St, Auckland. She towered like a gigantic hotel overlooking the whole town. Millie and I stepped ashore; my luggage, in the hold, went on to London.

NEW ZEALAND
SEPTEMBER 1969

The sign read:

GIRL FRIDAY WANTED URGENTLY

APPLY UPSTAIRS

Just a few blocks from where I had disembarked that morning in Auckland, I was changing money into New Zealand currency in a bank on Queens St.

There, on a side door, was the sign.

I couldn't resist seeing what it was all about. The teller explained that a very nice gentleman upstairs in an office went to the Cook Islands every week, taking people essentials. In exchange, they gave him shells and other items from their poor island.

I decided to investigate.

"I've come about the job," I said, a little breathless. I had carried my suitcase upstairs with me and entered the office across the hall. The sun streamed in through a skylight onto a chaos of papers, tapes, coffee cups, all in various stages of disuse. A half smoked cigar balanced precariously in the ashtray; its plume of smoke partly hid its owner.

A fat little man with a ruddy expression, wearing thick glasses, a brown T-shirt and shorts beamed at me as he stood behind the desk.

"Can you type, take messages, and use the telex machine?" I nodded in assent to each one. "Right, when can you start?" I did not have time to answer.

""I need someone for four weeks. My girl's had her baby. Little girl came early. She will be back in a month or so."

"What do you do here?"

"I'll tell you what I do. I have a small ship we take over to the Cook Islands every week. Bring their staples over, you know, batteries, butter, you name it. They send the orders in here. I go out and collect the goods and load them at Pier 3. I need someone here while I go out shopping." He grinned. "Could you do that?" his warm attitude was welcome enough. I could understand his predicament.

"I'd like to work for you but I've only just got off the ship from Sydney. I don't have anywhere to stay yet."

"That's easy- the YWCA. It's a couple of hundred yeards down the street, on this side. I hear it's quite comfortable. Go and get booked in there, drop off your case and I'll see you in a couple of hours, if you can make it. I'll pay you well. How's that?"

"Alright." I spoke hesitantly, but I was excited. "Thanks, Mr....?"

"Oh, name's Bob Burgess. Burgess Enterprises. And yours is?"

"Veronica Murray; I'm from England, Wimbledon. Tennis, you know." He nodded. "I just wanted to see something of New Zealand before leaving the Southern Hemisphere," I laughed.

"Good on yer, Ronnie. Tell you what; there are busses that go from Auckland to all over, you can do a lot of sightseeing on the weekends from here and still work during the week. I'll fit in with your plans as best I can."

"Thanks Bob, sounds like fun. I'll be right back."

Two Australian girls staying at the 'Y' decided to come with me one weekend, down to the hot springs at Roturua, in the south of the North Island. It was one of my many long New Zealand weekends. Bob let me off work at noon on Friday and I didn't work again until Tuesday.

We visited Lake Taupo, a huge expanse of mineral water surrounded by conifer trees and eucalyptus groves. In the same area there were geysers bubbling, hissing, and exploding steam at regular intervals. The air smelled of sulfur. It was wonderful to swim in the warm foaming water of the lake, and watch the hot geysers with temperatures near freezing outside. It was another matter to get out. We dashed inside to the dressing rooms, searching for our warm clothes. We booked a youth hostel close by. The meals were plain but we could have eaten anything.

"Our houses are heated by the hot springs," the locals told us. The ground around shook constantly. The Maoris demonstrated how they could fry an egg on the ground beside the hot water spouts. It was all a little disconcerting, surely the whole place could 'blow up' at any moment, but it was an adventure. We weren't scared.

In the evening we watched a Maori group sing, dance, and play their traditional melodies for us. The girls were petite and so graceful with flowers in their long dark hair. They were scantily dressed in grass skirts which switched as they swayed and twirled to the music. They used poi balls on long strings during their dances, entwining them and gracefully untwining them. Their musicians kept our feet tapping time under the midnight blue sky, full of twinkling stars.

We drank some of the white concoction they offered us, made from papayas, coconuts, and other fruit juices. Our eyes brightened; soon we were dancing too.

It was a wonderful time with sweet, friendly people. Language was not a hindrance. Most people spoke English; the local people spoke a form of Pilipino.

The Maoris, I discovered, were well assimilated into society in New Zealand, some even held places in Parliament. They were priests and doctors too. This was such a contrast with the Aborigines in Australia, who appeared to have no way of becoming part of modern society.

Back to work in Auckland. Bob Burgess had enjoyed offering suggestions for sightseeing trips, always keen to know how I found everything.

Six fascinating weeks went by, and then one day Bob informed me his secretary was ready to return to work. This was my opportunity to pack up and seek out more of this lovely country. I decided to take the train down to Wellington.

Memories of Mt Egmont, the highest mountain in the North Island, covered in snow, of BBQing rainbow trout abundant in every stream and Maori melodies all lingered with me as I left.

I had said good-bye to Bob Burgess and my friends at the 'Y' with a heavy heart.

Windy and wet, Wellington lived up to its name. Here I met Ann, who worked at Canterbury University. We played croquet on manicured lawns there, surrounded by a Victorian setting. We drank tea and ate cucumber sandwiches in the Clubhouse, just as I imagined the colonials had always done. Ann found a temporary office job for me at the University.

I learned Scottish dancing at the Saturday night 'hop,' which happened to be in the YWCA where I was staying once more. Crowds of folks from all around came into town for those evenings. They arrived dressed in tartans, flinging themselves into reels with abandon, excited by the piper's tunes. Their proud Scottish ancestry was in no danger of being forgotten; it was a wild time. I was glad of two things: I lived in the building, and the next day was Sunday- I could sleep in until Mass.

After a few weeks being blown about, often soaked by the rain (it is winter, I would tell myself as I shivered on my way), my temporary office job ended. Time to move on.

I took the ferry across to the South Island. There were pods of whales cavorting around us as we progressed through the island straits. We all watched, fascinated.

"Are you crossing for the first time?" asked an elderly women standing beside her husband.

"Yes, I'm going down to Christchurch to see the sights. I'm working my way round New Zealand."

"My husband and I live in Christchurch. Our daughter is about your age. She'll be coming to meet us, would you like to meet her?"

"I'd love to. I don't know anyone in Christchurch." We talked for a while.

"You could stay with us for a few days if you like. Our daughter, Meg, has traveled to Europe; she would enjoy telling you about her trip." I could not believe my luck.

Their car was parked dockside. "Here's Meg now." She was a slight blond with highly colored complexion. Her hair bounced in its ponytail was she hurried to meet her parents. There were hugs and kisses and laughter. I was introduced to Meg. I took to her immediately. She thought it would be great if I stayed with them.

"I was in London last year; went over with a working visa, I got back a month ago."

We drove for about two hours to Christchurch down the coast road. There were rugged cliffs, with lively rollers drawn towards them, bursting on the rocky base. I saw sandy beaches, abandoned by tourists this time of year, and sheep all over the hillsides. We passed a few small villages. How could so few people live in this idyllic setting, I thought. It was drawing towards evening as we drew into a shingled driveway and bumped towards the house.

It was a modern red brick home, with what appeared to be a field at the side and back. More sheep. It felt cozy inside the house. A fire glowed in the Rayburn stove. My cheeks burned with the sudden warmth. Meg and I made up the spare bed.

Next day we all went to church- it was Sunday. Meg showed me round town. Later we drove beside the Avon River, its banks thick with daffodils in bud, crocuses and anemones.

"The river weaves right through our town," Meg told me. We bobbed over several wooden bridges, down narrow streets, on the left hand side, just like in England.

"This country is gorgeous," I exclaimed. "Look there's snow on the hills up there. Yesterday we drove across areas of the moorland, like in Yorkshire. The gardens are just like home too, with all the flowers. Ducks and swans on the river remind me of the banks of the Thames."

"Have you noticed all the sheep here in New Zealand?" she asked. I nodded. "There are three sheep to each person here. We send whole shiploads to England in refrigerated containers."

We sat and discussed many things, how New Zealanders think of Britain as home. "Even if they were born here," Meg laughed.

I stayed with Meg and her parents for a couple days, then I told Meg, "Meg, I have enjoyed your hospitality. It's been wonderful; you've been so kind and helpful. You have made my stay so interesting. Now, I want to go down to Invercargill, then over to Milford Sound and see some of the snowy areas."

"You could take the train across Arthur's Pass then go north the Gracechurch from the west of the island."

With this information from Meg and a bus schedule in my hand, I said good-bye.

During the next few weeks, I saw some of the most beautiful scenery in the world. I joined a tour and relaxed as a modern bus carried me into the south of the South Island, where researchers leave to go study the Antarctic regions. At the tourist area of Milford Sound, the fresh snow covered the little villages around a lake. The mountains reminded me of the Alps. Our trip included driving to the summit of Mt Cook, the highest mountain in New Zealand.

We stayed at the 'Heritage Resort' up there. Being surrounded by pristine shimmering snow made us all feel elated.

When the tour ended some days later, I found the steam train that would take me to the top of Arthur's Pass. Once at the top, we were politely told to disembark. We waited, while our train reversed back down the glacier. Eventually another train came up from Gracechurch on the West Coast, and took us down to yet another fascinating part of New Zealand.

As the train trundled down to Gracechurch, I sat next to an Irish sister who was living in a convent in town. She insisted I stay at their convent for the night. I was given the visiting priest's room. We arrived late on Sunday afternoon. It was dark and raining. Soon, there was a knock on the door and the Reverend Mother came in with the little sister who had brought me. They brought trays in with them and we all had high tea. My travel story was told once again.

"Glory be to goodness, isn't it a wonderful t'ing you're after doing." Reverend Mother was Irish too.

She offered to put me on the bus to Picton in the morning when she went into town. There I could take the ferry back to the north Island once more.

A day on the smart, fast, electric train and I was once again in Auckland.

Getting out of New Zealand took some time. I spent a weekend with Millie and her family. She came with me into town to get my airline ticket. The travel office informed me I could not take New Zealand money out of the country. Mille had the answer: "Let's go shopping!"

We hit the Courts clothing store in Queens St and acted like teenagers, trying everything on. Soon my New Zealand cash disappeared. At the same bank I had entered on my first morning in Auckland, I bought traveler's checks, said good-bye to Bob Burgess and headed for the airport.

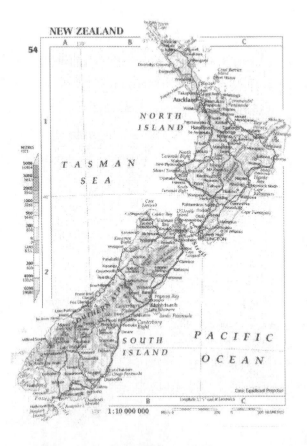

PART THREE

*

THE NEW WORLD

NEW ZEALAND TO THE US
OCTOBER, 1969

Our Qantas flight had left Auckland, New Zealand on time with few people on board. During the scheduled stop in Honolulu on route to San Francisco, the pilot had been alerted to a malfunction in one of the engines. The Qantas Representative explained with regret this meant a layover until the next day.

There were two couples traveling together. The wives were especially anxious to hear about my travels, as they had gone to England and Europe when they were students and had had such a pleasant time meeting helpful people. They wished to offer a helping hand to me.

"You cannot go back to London without seeing San Francisco," Marilyn cried loudly as we waited in the airport lounge. We discussed the delay, agreeing we couldn't do anything about it. They asked me to sit with them at dinner in the Presidents' Hotel where we were taken for the night.

We were served one tropical delicacy after another: shellfish, salad with coconut, ginger flavored savory delights, accompanied by some fine wines. Conversation flowed freely. We became firm friends. I guessed they were in their late forties. Both women were cleverly dressed in fine style, their hairdos impeccable. They wore expensive leather shoes. The men, wearing dark city suits, carried large briefcases.

They were interested to hear about my travels. I learned that their homes were in Marin County, an exclusive area north of San Francisco. What I did not know was that I was eating with two highly successful men in the American business world, who had taken their wives to New Zealand for the opening of the latest hydro-electric dam in the South Island which their Company had just completed.

After dinner my new friends and I enjoyed a good night's rest. Back on board another plane we spent several more hours relaxing and chatting like old friends. Eventually, landing in San Francisco, my friends bade me goodbye after giving me their phone numbers and making sure I had somewhere to stay.

I decided to stay at the YWCA on Sutter Street. The notice board had several interesting prospects for jobs I noticed. The room I was given had a fire door leading out on to the balcony from which I looked down onto the busy street. It was early evening and I was fascinated to see people rushing along with shopping bags, some with small children, scurrying home to dinner. I turned to go back into my room. I knew nothing about fire doors. I was firmly locked out in my robe as I had just taken a shower. I banged on the door and called down to the impervious world below. It was getting dark. Eventually a very annoyed woman came out and we reentered the room. I was shaken up but the woman berated me for going outside. Had I not seen the notice?

Back down in the lounge I reread an advertisement by an elderly lady for someone to stay in her home at night as she was nervous on her own. I telephoned. A woman with a German sounding accent answered. She told me my days would be free. I would not have to pay rent and she was on the bus route. She convinced me I was really needed so I left the YWCA, and took the bus. I should have seen a red light when I asked the driver to let me off at a certain stop in the Potrero district. "Are you sure you want to get off here"? He asked. It was raining but I didn't have far to go. What astonished me was seeing group of children strolling down the roads wearing mostly white sheets and carrying large bags. It was Halloween. It was my first encounter with the American tradition of 'trick or treating.'

Mrs. Neumann was pleasant enough. My room had a large bed in it, not leaving much room for my belongings. The furniture was old with a large dresser in front of the window. Leaving my room, I decided to walk down the neighborhood and find the shops. Mrs. Neumann rushed out of her room, asking where I was going. I told her, "To find the shops."

"Oh no," she cried, "It's not safe to go alone and now it's late. Go tomorrow morning and I will go with you." And this we did. Fortunately I had eaten earlier and Mrs. Neumann gave me a cup of tea and cookies.

That night I discovered a rash on my torso. It hurt and itched. As I had noticed a hospital close by, I went out early the next morning to get identification for my spots. I joined a long line of the poorest souls with strings of children who looked as if they had waited all night. It was very unpleasant and after an hour or so I left. A girl I had met at the YWCA who was a nurse had given me her phone number. When I called her, she told me, "You've got shingles. Go to a doctor." I told her that I naturally had no doctor, whereupon she told me to call her doctor and explain that I had no insurance and little money. The kind doctor saw me the next day, confirmed I had shingles and said, "I could prescribe expensive medicine but the best thing is to keep bathing the area in warm salt water." He only charged me ten dollars.

Mrs. Neumann lived in the Portuguese area of San Francisco. I discovered this on Sunday when I got up to go to church. I heard a language unlike any I had ever heard in Europe- it was Portuguese. The people were all dressed for Sunday; the men in white shirts and black pants, the women and children wore pretty outfits, some carrying flowers. They were very happy and talked excitedly. However, that night there was a huge explosion. Later, I discovered a man had had a fight with his wife and turned the gas taps on and lit a match. That happened only a couple of houses from where I was staying. I left Mrs. Neumann and took the bus back into San Francisco.

There was a message from my friends from the air trip. When I called them, they came and took me out for the day and back to their home for dinner.

Another morning I walked by an employment agency and casually looked at the advertisements. Out of curiosity, I talked to one of the ladies inside. She got excited when I told her about my travels. She said, "I have the perfect place for you! It is to speak

English with a little girl of six years. Her parents work and their housekeepers are all Spanish speaking. They live well in a very nice neighborhood. I can take you there." I replied, "I don't have a visa and I am late getting home to England." She argued and I went with her into the lap of luxury to Hillsborough.

I spent two weeks in that house. The man of the house was a successful businessman and his wife had her own plane. The little daughter, Mary, had so many after-school activities, such as tennis lessons, ballet, etc. which she went to with her next door friend, another Mary. I hardly saw the child and spent time helping the Mexican housekeeper. My memories are of changing the white gold initialed towels each morning and of making salad each evening, pulling the leaves apart by hand. The family was preparing to go their house on the seventeenth hole at Pebble Beach, by which time they wanted me in uniform. I said that job was not what I wanted and we parted on amicable terms.

THE JOB THAT CHANGED MY LIFE

This time when I returned to my San Francisco residence, I called my travel friends and told them I would be leaving. "Oh no," my lady friend exclaimed, "My husband is arranging a job for you in his company. I have been trying to contact you. He said you are to go down to his office in the morning."

"But I don't have a visa," I replied, "And I am late going home anyway."

"Don't worry about anything; just go. Here is the address; ask for Marion."

The position I was to have was settling families who would travel overseas with their husbands/fathers for perhaps two years. I would manage their medicals, injections, housing enquiries, schools for children and generally make them feel happy about the move and the experience they would have. Marion took me across the street to the Immigration Office where I was handed a preliminary letter saying my green card would be in the mail.

I took the job.

That was it. Was I dreaming? I sat down and wrote my sister a long letter; she was going to be upset I wasn't coming home after all.

How could I explain how kind everyone had been and how I now felt obligated to stay, at least for a while? Would she please explain this to my friend Joyce, and ask her to continue to look after my house for me?

As I walked along Bush Street after my interview with Marion, I passed the French church and went inside to pray for guidance; I was starting a new life in America. I continued my walk and caught sight of a 'Vacancy' sign outside one of the many private hotels. I saw there was a French restaurant inside and decided to investigate. French cuisine would be a delightful change. It smelled good too.

My lunch was served by Michelle, the lady of the house who explained, in a strong French accent that she, her husband and her brother ran the hotel, her brother being the cook. They had taken over the building which was in need of repair and gradually, as they completely refurbished each room they rented it out. Most of the people, she said, worked in town and came home at night for dinner. She also served breakfast. Michelle showed me the room on the ground floor with a tiny bathroom. The rent was reasonable so I said I would move in; it was within walking distance from my new job.

The people I became acquainted with at the hotel were employed mostly in large engineering and building companies. At the weekend, they would often carpool to one of the beautiful areas outside the city. I was invited and found life to be very pleasant. My new job was a challenge. Americans spelled words differently from my English schooling. Work started eight o'clock a.m. - so early!

After a few weeks in San Francisco, I now had a very fine job with a good boss but I had not made many friends. When I heard the office would be closed for four days at Christmas I decided to fly down to Los Angeles to see another American city.

When I look back I wonder how I did it. Someone told me of an inexpensive hotel in downtown LA and on Christmas Eve, after work, I arrived at the hotel about nine p.m. having had an uneventful flight and found the hotel shuttle waiting for me.

The receptionist was most helpful. I asked about Midnight Mass nearby and she informed me St. Viviana's Cathedral was not far away and that another girl had already booked a taxi to go there and suggested we might go together. At eleven p.m. I met the other girl and we became acquainted. She was traveling as well. She told me that she was going to Disney Land the next day, and asked if I would like to go along. It seemed a good idea as I had no other plans.

Arriving at the cathedral early, we were able to sit and watch others arrive, until the place was full. Besides it being a High Mass with many priests, the cardinal was the main celebrant. However, the most unexpected treat was a quartet from the opera house which sang the Mass. It was a most wonderful experience for the two of us.

As we left the cathedral, our taxi driver found us and took us back to the hotel.

Jan, my new friend, and I had arranged to meet at nine a.m. and having had a hurried breakfast boarded the bus for what would be a most incredible day at Disney Land. We were greeted by Mickey Mouse and escorted to where a huge parade was to take place, with color and glitter of which I had never imagined. As it was Christmas Day, all kinds of treats were offered to those who chose that day to visit Walt Disney's dreamland.

It was late when we two travelers returned to our hotel. Jan was flying out of LA the next day, so we said good-bye and I decided to go down to the new Music Conservatory. I discovered it was possible to walk around inside and step into the concert halls where rehearsals were taking place. Imagine my surprise when the conductor of the orchestra, wearing a bright blue pullover, turned around and I recognized him as Yehudi Menuin. Naturally I sat there, an audience of one, and enjoyed the most wonderful music concert. Some of the time Mr. Menuin conducted and other times he played his violin. When the rehearsal was over I was hungry and to my delight discovered there was a coffee shop in the Music Conservatory where I enjoyed lunch. A walk down Sunset Boulevard concluded my day. Next morning I flew back to San Francisco, from where I had left, wondering what lonely Christmas I might have had; but it had been wonderful.

When I returned to work I related my enjoyable Christmas to my boss, his reply being "That's great! You have another long weekend coming up for New Years; what will you do?"

My friend Tony from Sydney, Australia had told me of a cousin of his living in Palo Alto. "You should contact him. He and his wife would love to meet you." So that is what I did.

I telephoned Phil that evening. Tony had written to them telling them to expect a call from me. "We are having a party for New Years," Phil exclaimed excitedly, "Will you come? Let us know what train you will be on and Frances-my wife- or I will meet you. Stay over for the weekend! Our son will be home from college."

I agreed and when I arrived at Palo Alto station a neat, pretty, petite older lady found me and introduced herself as Frances. We talked incessantly as we drove to their lovely home beside Stanford University. On arrival, Frances took me into the music room where Phil greeted me warmly. There were two harpsichords here: one large with a full-size keyboard, the other a smaller spinet. "I made these," Phil said proudly, "from a kit. The small one is the size J.S. Bach composed on." The keys were black and white, but in reverse of normal pianos. He played a few bars on each instrument as I expressed my amazement at his prowess. On a card table nearby were many empty bottles, each with a slip of paper in the top. "What are they for?" I asked.

"Oh, you'll see later," he laughed.

After a while I met their son Tom and we chatted over a snack. Then people started to arrive for the party; mostly young male friends of Tom. Later, some colleagues of Phil came in and he introduced me to Dennis who I noticed had come alone. He and I talked for a while about Stanford, where I learned he was a professor.

About nine o'clock Phil announced it was rehearsal time. He brought in the table with the bottles on and gave everyone a bottle. Each one had a printed musical note on it. We gathered around while

Phil explained that we had to blow across the mouth of the bottle. Loud bursts of unmelodic sounds came forth. Phil then moved us- all twenty-five partners- until we were formed into a scale. He then taught us to play 'Old Lang Syne' on our bottles.

We took a couple of breaks to 'wet our whistles' and then it was near midnight. We waited for the chimes of the New Year and then we performed our incredible rendition of 'Old Lang Syne'. It was great fun and we applauded Phil for his magnificent achievement.

Being new to the U.S. I had no idea what New Year's Day would bring. When I eventually joined the family for a late breakfast, the T.V. was on loudly and not much attention was paid to anything else. It was Football Day.

The noise and the bright colors of the uniforms on the huge screen gave me a headache and I walked outside. I was joined by Dennis who had come round earlier. Frances suggested he take me to visit Stanford University. I had the grand tour inside and outside the campus. It was drizzling with rain but it did not dampen my impression of the magnificent edifice.

By mid-afternoon the games were still going lustily but most of the viewers were napping. Frances took me to her sewing room and showed me her hobby, which was lapidary. She had some beautiful stones made into bracelets, rings and necklaces. She had a veritable workshop of tools, strands of wire and boxes of clasps. I was very impressed. She told me there was an exhibition of lapidary work in a nearby town that she would like to take me to the next day. As I had to get back to San Francisco by the evening, we agreed she would drop me off at the station after we had viewed the exhibition.

Thus, after an intriguing morning learning how semi-precious stones were cut, polished and mounted and after a classic seafood lunch at Mings, I returned to San Francisco ready to relate my adventures of my first New Year in the U.S.

I MEET ART

It was not long before I met Art. He used to serve breakfast before going to college (on his G.I. Bill). He had a room on the sixth floor of the Cornell where I was staying. However, he seldom came with the rest of the group on our weekend adventures. Later I discovered he went home to Palo Alto where his mother, grandfather and sister lived. We dated during the week. Then he asked if I would like to visit his family at the weekend.

Art's family made me feel welcome and I came to know many other members of his charming family. This became another home for me. Grandad loved to play Scrabble after dinner and I would join him, playing for hours some evenings.

The home on Tennyson Avenue, Palo Alto was not large but was well-appointed with shiny wood floors and an elegant stairway. The main front room was off the front door and one side was the dining area and the other a cozy lounge. The kitchen was little more than a galley, behind which was Grandad's bed sitting room. When Art was small, the garden backed on to a farm but now more gardens led to homes in the next street. The house had three bedrooms upstairs, the master bedroom having a small doorway leading to attic space. Art's mother slept downstairs in a small room off the lounge.

When I first met Mary, Art's mother, she was about to retire from a long career at Stanford Children's Hospital. Definitely an organizer, she took great care of the house, especially of the white rug that covered most of the front room. She talked, naming names, of different cleaners and trades people whom she employed on a regular basis and whom Art had known for years. Fortunately she liked me, as did his sister Betsy who came home at the weekends from her digs in San Francisco, near the bank where she worked.

Art didn't own a car in San Francisco, but on the weekends he used his mother's old Mercedes to show me around his beautiful neighborhood. As our relationship grew, we spent more and more weekends in Palo Alto. I began to feel like one of the family.

When Art's engineering college course ended he asked me to marry him. He had acquired a job with Motorola, working in the San Francisco area. While he was not Catholic, I did not hesitate to accept his offer. I had been praying about our relationship, and it seemed the right and sensible thing to do. We were married in the Newman Center chapel of Stanford University. The officiator was Fr. Durie and the organist a music scholar from the school.

My sister's best friend Mel had married an American and they lived in Sacramento. Her husband Joe gave me away and Mel was my matron of honor. We also invited the French couple from our hotel. All the other attendees were Art's family and friends. It was May, 1970.

Back at our hotel in San Francisco, the French couple had reorganized things for us. My room was now equipped with a kitchen corner and there was now a large double bed. This French couple was delighted for us and did all they could to make us comfortable. However, their English was not the best. We had had to smile when along with their gift of a coffee percolator was a sympathy card. However, the words on the card fitted the occasion perfectly: "At this special time our thoughts are with you."

Our love nest at the Cornell Residential Hotel, although comfortable and convenient, was too small. We needed our own place. After a couple of months, we moved to an apartment nearby. Frequently we would go over to the Cornell to have dinner with our old friends.

Our weekends were spent mostly in Palo Alto with Art's family. I soon learned that sports took precedence over almost anything in that household. Even meals were arranged to coincide with half-time. I tried my best to understand American football and baseball, but it was not easy. If I asked a question it would possibly be ignored, so intense was the concentration on the game. The postmortem analysis after the game often lasted through dinner. Grandad would then come to my aid, suggesting a game of Scrabble. They were happy times.

In October of that same year, 1970, I left Art, who could not get time off work, to travel to London to see my family and check on my house in Wimbledon, which was being taken care of my friend Joyce. She had two renters living there with her, one of them my friend whose apartment I had shared in Sydney. Maureen Shannon had come to London on a year's working permit.

There was no spare bedroom; I slept on a couch in the dining room. The first week after my arrival was spent with my sister down in Sussex. It was so good to meet up once more with my good friends; we talked non-stop.

I had also planned, before I had left for Australia, to go to Oberammergau, Austria in 1970 with several other friends. We would all meet there, from wherever life had led us, at the appointed time.

Every ten years, a Passion Play of enormous dimensions, taking all day to unfold, is enacted in this mountain village of Austria. With a cast of hundreds, preparation takes a minimum of one year. The villagers act all the parts; the bartender could be playing Judas or the baker, Peter. Mary could be a local girl just out of school.

The play takes place in the open air, with canvas overhead for inside scenes, where appropriate. The audience is also outside. While the weather was fine the day we attended the pageant, there were stories of robes having to be dried out at intermissions on rainy days. The play is a worldwide attraction; our group was only able to stay in the area for two nights, one before and one after the play, so that the next group of tourists could come into town.

The townsfolk were very talented. Besides their acting abilities, they made beautifully carved local wood, paintings and ceramic artifacts for sale. Murals covering the walls of homes, some two stories high, shone like stained glass in a cathedral.

Our accommodation was with a local family who gave us a warm welcome, including delicious German food. Everyone spoke some English. We slept under immense eiderdown quilts on feather mattresses- a luxurious sensation, to say the least.

The experience in Oberammergau was unique; an unforgettable few days. Back in England, I visited with my brothers and their families. Then I went back to Sussex to my sister and her family, who took me to the airport for my flight back to San Francisco.

PETALUMA, 1972

On my return home I discovered that Art had spent a weekend with his school friends, who had moved up to Petaluma, about forty miles north of San Francisco. Soon, he took me up to meet Norm, his wife and two children. Thereafter, we spent several weekends with them in a peaceful, rural setting where nothing seemed to be more important than enjoying each day in glorious farm country surrounded by green hills.

We started looking at houses for sale.

"Honey, how do we get to work from here?" I asked Art.

Norman, our host responded, "There are express busses that leave early in the morning, about six thirty I think, and get to San Francisco by eight o'clock."

Our faces lit up. "That would be perfect," we answered in unison.

Soon we talked to an elderly man, Duke, who owned a small real estate business in Petaluma. He explained how the little city was growing. More people were commuting to work in San Francisco, but the house prices were still low. He added, "I'm going to court next week, over a house that is an estate property. It's quite small- two bedrooms, just up the hill here." He pointed across the way. "It needs some work, but the family isn't interested in it. I think ten thousand dollars is the minimum they'll take. Come and look at it."

It had a porch with gables situated on a corner high above town. We walked under two shady walnut trees down the path to the front door. Although sadly neglected, lofty ceilings and wood floors greeted us inside. Down the hall which had rooms on each side, we came into a large country kitchen with a pantry. There were expansive views over the countryside from the front room and over town from the kitchen. A Wedgewood gas and wood burning stove stood along one wall, bearing several fascinating dials that seemed to smile at me. That was it; I went to find Art.

I could hear voices from the master bedroom. "Duke, she loves it. How could we negotiate with the court?"

"You'd have to be in court with me. Then, when the estate comes before the judge he will say, 'Do I have a bid higher than ten thousand dollars?' At that point, you would say that you have an offer."

I burst in. "You can't get time off work, Art. Could I do it? It's easier for me to get away."

"Sure," our friend answered, "I'll pick you up Thursday morning." I couldn't sleep waiting for Thursday.

Eventually, we were seated in court in good time. Duke briefed me as he looked around. "I don't see any competition; you're in luck."

The judge asked the exact question "Will anyone offer more than ten thousand dollars for this property?"

I rose up nervously. "Ten thousand five hundred, sir."

There were no more bids. I wrote a check for ten percent of the amount and rushed home to call Art.

Two weeks later, we moved in.

Like two small birds, we worked on our nest. Soon it gleamed from our hard labors; the wood floors shone, the wood burning stove sent warmth through the house. Art painted on the weekends, adding tiny gold touches to the white Victorian cornices, elaborately decorated with rosebuds. In the pantry, the glass cupboard doors soon displayed jars of pickles, canned fruits, and jam given to us by our kind neighbors when they came to welcome us. A tall dresser displayed my pretty china from England.

Our kitchen table was a thick piece of plywood, painted white, on which I had glued autumn leaves from a trip we had taken to Canada. A coat of clear hard varnish protected the top.

Once the essential decorating was complete, we went on expeditions to the cheese factory, the egg ranch, but especially to Tamales Bay to pick up oysters. Then there were trips to the vineyards dotted all over the hills. We watched as the smudge pots were lit when frost threatened in the winter evenings.

Our walnut harvest was messy; the green outer shells harbored tannin brown oil that stained everything, but the nuts were unbeatable. Some were even salted, left out in the sun for weeks then pickled.

Art worked in the garden, untended for many years, amassing an expanse of zinnias, delphiniums, geraniums, and wild flowers all over the two corners of the street, and he repaired and painted the white picket fence. People passing by stopped to admire the flowers; it was a picture.

One terrible night that picture was shattered, as were our nerves. About one a.m. we were awakened by a loud crash that shook the house. This was followed by several smaller bangs, then silence. We rushed from our bed. There, on the front porch, was a young motorcyclist in a black leather jacket. He appeared unconscious.

"You better call 911, Honey. He looks bad." My teeth chattered as I spoke.

"Don't you touch him. Let the paramedics see to him." He called 911.

It appeared he had missed the corner, traveling too fast, and careened up on to our lawn, gouging out a deep ridge as he went. Mounting the steps, he was hurled against our front door, before parting from his bike. He was not wearing a helmet.

The next day, the bike was removed while we were at work. The hospital, when we called, informed us that he had been released, but we were unable to get any more information; even his name remained a mystery.

Art repaired the damage to our front yard, but we will never forget the terror of that night.

Petaluma had a special charm which we loved. Sadly we weren't able to be involved in the town's activities; there was so little spare time. When we ate out, the selection of restaurants with variable specialties was endless. Quaint local shops made us inquisitive to venture inside.

Our bus left town at six-thirty every morning. We learned how to enter quietly, as the passengers who were coming from Santa Rosa, farther north, were all asleep. No one spoke; it was like a dormitory after lights out.

In the summer getting up early was fine, but the second winter was awful. It was very wet, and the bus we traveled in leaked. It became customary to put our umbrellas up inside the bus as we bumped along through Marin County, then over the Golden Gate Bridge to our destination. Some days when the Russian River flooded over the road, we couldn't get through. The bus was then turned around, taking us back to Petaluma.

We both felt the strain of the long workdays, especially because Art's communications job required him to be on twenty-four hour call every other week. When he was called, possibly at three a.m., he would have to drive forty miles to one of the facilities in the San Francisco area, wherever the communication breakdown had occurred. Having dealt with the emergency, he would often go straight to work to complete his daily duties there.

The following summer, we took a vacation in England, so that Art could meet my family. My house in Wimbledon was full of renters, some from Australia whom I had invited, thinking I would be home. We stayed with my brother in Surrey and my sister in Sussex.

It was a marvelous three weeks, during which my dear husband fell crazily in love with England. The weather enhanced the countryside with sunshine almost daily. He even liked walking in the rain. Our family made sure we were shown the prettiest countryside, given the best food, taken to the best pubs; in other words, we were spoiled rotten.

"Let's see what the house prices are like here," he said, pouring over the advertisements in the real estate office windows. I was ecstatic; I had been away from England for too long.

We traveled for miles all over southern England, from Kent to Cornwall, in a state of euphoria, searching for the impossible: a house with land that we could afford. We even considered a farmhouse, or rather two knocked into one, in Cornwall in a hamlet called Frithle Stockstone. It had twenty-five acres of land with sheep and cows. At that time there was a special low tax on arable land. We looked at a cottage built on three levels on a steep hill overlooking the Severn River, near Wales. Prices were low, but we weren't ready to buy.

Our vacation ended but we knew, as we sat in a plane going over the Atlantic, that it would not be long before we returned.

Back in Petaluma, we talked once more with our friend Duke about real estate. Not long after, he brought to our house a young musician in his twenties, dressed in a shiny black leather coat and tight jeans. He danced around our little nest, humming with pleasure. In the kitchen he brought out his checkbook. "How much did you say the price was?"

His price was for the amount we asked, double what we paid two years earlier.

We were in shock. I wrote home to tell the family what had happened and that we would be coming home to live. In response, we were told that our two single aunts who had lived at our grandparent's home had been taken to a retirement home, leaving that house vacant. It was in great need of repair, and it was decided we should live there. Art would take care of the renovation of the house.

Within a month we said goodbye to our lovely little nest, left our jobs, and put our belongings on a train to Savannah, Georgia, from where they were to be shipped off to London.

We also went by train across America, taking the southern route: through Los Angeles, Huston, Avery Island (where the tabasco plant is grown), and Montgomery, Alabama, where we crossed bridges over the Mississippi River. It was in full flood, leaving poor areas of shanty homes knee deep in water. The area looked starkly deserted.

Sleeping in the train in a long carriage with the lights dimmed wasn't too uncomfortable. The seats were adjustable, with footrests. We were given pillows and a blanket.

In the early morning, we smelled coffee brewing. Art left and returned with two steaming cups of coffee. He snapped the vacant seat in front of us to its upright position to get by. Unfortunately, it caught and hurled his hot coffee across the aisle, on to the back of a large African American lady who was bending over her luggage. She was dressed in white, with gloves and a smart hat. She screamed, not knowing what had happened. Art assured her it was an accident.

"Oh my, oh my!" she cried. Then she asked, "Has my dress been stained?" We busied ourselves with damp towels, trying to remove what was an already established long brown stain. We bought her breakfast; she still seemed stunned. She left the train at the next station.

Art's cousin, Jeff, met us in Savannah, where we enjoyed a week's vacation, hiring bicycles to venture out into the back country, discovering the fascinating history of the area. We marveled at huge old oak trees meeting high above us on the road, dripping with moss. We saw cotton, picked and stacked in great railroad trucks, waiting to be transported for processing. There were wide expanses of land around gracious plantation houses, built centuries ago but still inhabited. We could almost hear the singing of the workers out in the endless fields of crops. There were gun placements, preserved from the Civil War, along with statues of the heroes of that time.

It was a grand, educational week; staying with Jeff, Brenda, and their two teenage daughters had enlightened us to a way of life in the south far different from our own.

We waved good-bye to our family from a train bound to New York. Next day we boarded a plane to London, to a new phase of our married life.

LONDON, 1974-1976

We could not have known that the next few years would bring an economic recession to the British Isles, making life in England extremely hard. It was a time of political change, from a mildly conservative government to a very liberal and socialistic one. Taxes soared, giving no incentive to earn a living. Elevated interest rates led to the highest cost of living the country had ever known. Gasoline was in short supply, as were most household commodities; even toilet rolls were rationed to one per person. Things were tough.

The British have a way of ridiculing difficult situations. Comedians had a great time, but not so the public, as they waited in line to get their quota of gasoline. The situation did not improve. Winter was an exceptionally cold one, with fair amounts of snow. Although most Britains put up with the inconveniences, Art didn't see the need.

The aunt's home in Wilton Crescent, Wimbledon, was situated in a quiet neighborhood close to a park, within walking distance to the railway station, by way of semi-rural area of pathways that ran behind homes and over a wide footbridge spanning the train lines. A further five minutes' walk led into the main thoroughfare of shops in Wimbledon Broadway. I noticed a great difference here. After all, I had not lived in Wimbledon for several years.

Many of the stores I had known before leaving England had disappeared. Brands, the butcher's shop had gone, as had Clarkes, the coffee shop and bakery. In their place stood food markets, selling everything from meat to vegetables to clothing.

I missed LeFerbres (LeFevers) Haberdashery store, with its rolls of fabric and household linins, where I had been taken to buy school uniforms. I especially missed the gadget on each counter where the salesperson put payments, then pulled a chord, sending the spool high above me over to the cashier in the corner of the store. She, having emptied the spool, would return it to our salesperson where it would arrive with a clonk, complete with change.

Kennards had gone; another general store which had specialized in household necessities as well as clothes, curtains, furniture and notions. There was a tea room upstairs complete with palms and aspidistras, from whose tables and chairs the bustle of the shop could be viewed at leisure. Two elderly ladies entertained on Saturdays; one with the piano, the other on violin. We never considered them good musicians; in fact some of their variations were painful and only the need to observe who was shopping prevented us from giving up a ringside seat. Imagine our astonishment at hearing these old girls had won the European Song Contest one year, with 'Cruising Down the River on a Sunday Afternoon.'

'Elys was still there, an exclusive clothing and beauty store where, as school girls walking home, my friends and I would cut through the store, pressing the scent testers as we went or trying on expensive hats, infuriating the sales ladies who hurried to put things straight the minute we left.

Art set to work repairing and painting the grand old four-bedroom Wilton Crescent house. It had large rooms with ceilings ten feet high and oak furniture and fireplaces sadly in need of oil and beeswax. The stairs to the second floor rose with an oak balustrade, curving at the top onto a tall square landing, off which were the heavy wooden doors into the bedrooms.

Quantities of regency striped wallpaper were measured and pasted. We moved from room to room, sleeping like Goldilocks in various high-backed beds as the work progressed. It took almost a year to complete the project.

We took time off to return to Cornwall to find our farmhouse, which had been for sale at $16,000 the year before. It had recently been sold for $40,000; the acreage had been split into building sites. We realized it had been an impossible dream. We were a sad couple driving home that day.

Driving round the countryside in an old Morris Minor, we looked at scores of other houses but things had become so expensive, it became obvious the market was beyond our means.

Wilton Crescent was to be sold and divided among the family. During the year one of my aunts had died; the other was not expected to live long, as she lay in a semi-conscious state in the nursing home.

It was America's Thanksgiving Day. We had invited all the family to the house for a celebrations dinner with turkey and all the trimmings. Art had spent hours on the telephone, to bakeries as far away as London, trying unsuccessfully to locate a pumpkin pie.

"No one seems to know what I'm talking about!" He sounded exasperated. "One lady remarked, 'Who do you think I am, Cinderella?'"

During dinner in the now elegant dining room, complete with the gold velvet drapes hiding the wintry scene outside, we discussed our situation with my sister and brothers. Although Art had a residence visa allowing him to work permanently in England, he found nothing that interested him bearing the salary he was used to. It became obvious that he should return to the United States, find a job and somewhere for us to live. I would follow later. Sadly, I explained, "It's easier for me to assimilate in America than it is for him to settle here."

No sooner had Art left, I made a terrible discovery. My American residence visa was out of date. Horrified, I learned I had to apply all over again to live and work in the United States, including an interview, medical examination, fingerprints, etc. This took some months, even though my visa was only three months out of date.

By the time I was informed I could leave for America, Art had secured a job and found a temporary home for us in Oregon, where his twin uncles lived, up on the Rogue River.

With mixed emotions and no little trepidation I waved goodbye to friends and family.

"Oregon, here I come," I whispered through my tears.

OREGON, 1976-1981

At three o'clock in the afternoon the phone rang.

"This is Gus down at the bus depot. The San Francisco bus just dropped off Mrs. Ayres' luggage. There's a ton of it- six trunks, several suitcases, and boxes. I can't move in here. Someone must come at once and remove it."

Since coming back to the States, Art had come up to stay with his Uncle Tom and Aunt Ellen in Gold Beach, Oregon. He managed to get hired at the plywood mill, working swing shift three to midnight. I had just flown back to America a couple days earlier, after our eighteen-month stay in England, coming into this idyllic yet strange household.

There was no way I could get in touch with Art at work. Reluctantly I approached Uncle Tom. "Would you please drive me down to town to pick up my luggage?"

Uncle Tom's ranch, built several years earlier by him and his wife Ellen, sat seventeen miles up the wild Rogue River on eleven acres, facing a wide turn on the river. The view was extensive and awesome.

Tom's identical twin brother, Dick, had also lived on this property since his retirement in a mobile home. The men were seventy years old when I first met them, like two peas in a pod; tall, willowy tough guys whose first vodka and orange juice came with their lunch and kept coming until bedtime.

Work on their eleven acres- tending to vegetable beds, fishing from the bank, feeding Dick's pet trout languishing in a pond he had built, or harnessing a stream from high up on the rocks above- would be completed by midday. They would then retreat to the couch on the veranda, gaze at the river, acknowledging through misty eyes the mail boat as it passed by. They knew most people on the river. Thus the lazy afternoons passed to the tune of hummingbirds, bees, and the occasional splash from the river as a salmon jumped or a boat went by.

Ellen stayed in the kitchen now family room of the cabin most of the time, cooking or preserving fruits, vegetables, fish, etc. She managed to keep up with the boys and their vodka; in fact she usually acted the barmaid. Then she would sit outside for a while in her rocking chair before resuming her chores inside.

Both men slowly and deliberately rose from their lounge chairs and made for the truck. Nothing was said. I followed.

Our speedy progress down the unpaved, curving, narrow road had me praying as I swayed between these two tall men. Then Tom stopped the vehicle, and without explanation got out, strolled round to the passenger's side, opened the door and mumbled "You drive" to his brother Dick. Also a man of few words, Dick climbed out, came round to the driver's side and hitched himself up into the cab. Tom eased his way in beside me. We traveled more slowly into town without incident.

I wondered how I would be able to load the heavy luggage onto the truck, remembering that both Tom and Dick had heart problems. Fortunately Gus started loading them up for me while the two men stood by.

"Dick, could you let me have a couple of dollars for Gus? I forgot my purse," I whispered.

"Oh, he doesn't need anything," came the miserly reply. I was so embarrassed.

On the way home in the early evening mist, as we rounded a corner we hit a deer. Tom, who was driving again, jumped out, producing a knife from his belt. Thinking the deer was near death, I presumed he would put it out of its misery. He approached the creature and, to my astonishment, gave it a hefty kick. It staggered to its feet and ran for cover off the road. It had just been stunned and was very much alive.

Tom slowly heaved himself up into the cab and gave a dry laugh; that was all. We drove on home in the growing dark.

Jan lived next to Tom on her own eleven acres. Art had known her from earlier visits to his uncle. He took me to visit her in her mobile home, looking over the river. I found a slightly built delightful elderly lady who exuded great personality. She and I became warm friends.

"My Joe was a guide for parties going fishing up the river. He built this great garage as a storage workshop for us. It's bigger than the house," she laughed.

"It looks wonderful for all your supplies; oh, you have a washer and dryer in here too! That's lovely. I suppose this work bench is what he used for cleaning the fish?" I asked.

She nodded. "Now I use it for anything and everything, since he passed away."

Behind the mobile home there was a thirty-two-foot trailer. Jan took us inside. "This here was specially converted by Joe. He was over six feet; he made the roof higher and the bed longer." Again she laughed; she spoke proudly about the alterations Joe had done.

"Now, if you and Art like, you could live here until you get settled with a proper home up here. What do you think?"

"Oh Jan, that would be terrific! It is so kind of you." The relief was audible in my voice. "It will give us somewhere to store our luggage too. We can cook here- look Art, the stove has four jets. I'll find some sheets-" I started to say.

"No, don't go opening up all your cases. Use my stuff while you're up here." I hugged her; so did Art.

We stayed with Jan for a couple months. Like genuine country folk, we walked to visit our neighbors from time to time to hear their news and sip a cool drink. Country living in the middle of summer in an idyllic situation was a blessing. There were huckleberries to be picked, along with blackberries and raspberries. Jan grew her own vegetables; there was plenty for us all. As I was at home all day while Art worked, Jan and I grew to be close friends.

Since her husband had died of cancer some ten years before leaving her alone on their eleven acres, Jan appeared to have become quite a hermit, going into town only a couple mornings a month, bringing back scores of books, reading anything and everything. To keep the wild grasses down around her property, she attacked them with a machete. Making sure her well and leach lines worked properly had made her a tough lady.

"I learned to be independent," she confided in me one day. "Being alone up here makes you determined to do things for yourself. Of course, the neighbors would help but I hate to bother them. No one from town would come out without it costing a small fortune, which I don't have," she chuckled. Her laugh was infectious and I soon settled down and relaxed.

Art and I went searching for a home, not knowing exactly what we wanted. We settled for a mid-size three-bedroom older rambler house on about an acre of land. The rear of the property was down a steep slope covered with ferns and brambles with a pond at the bottom. Soon we had ducks on the pond, together with muskrats. These are creatures similar to beavers and certainly as large. They have thick leathery tails which help them to swim and navigate the waterways.

There were two apartments included in the property. Both were rented; it seemed like this would be a great asset to help us pay the mortgage. The property, situated high up on the top of a hill, was within walking distance of town. We could see and hear the ocean and the sea lions.

The house itself was quite substantial and livable, with three bedrooms, a separate dining room, off which was a tiny room into which I squeezed my piano. This became my study, where I typed, sang, sewed, and enjoyed the greenhouse outside. This Art built, so that even on stormy days we could work on our plants. In there we also put an incubator with the intention of raising baby ducks, but they seemed to manage on their own. The greenhouse acted as a solar warming factor, making my study very cozy on those winter days.

The rear of the house was unfinished, needing insulation, hardboard and finishing. The back bathroom housed the washing machine and dryer.

We moved in on the first day it rained that winter. The coast of Oregon has one hundred inches of rain every year, but during June, July, August, and sometimes September, there is only the occasional wet day. When the winter storms came, the wind was ferocious and the rain blew sideways. I would sit and watch the large windowpanes dip in and out. This frightened me and I would hurry to close the drapes in case the windows blew in.

It was fortunate that Art worked at the mill from three to midnight, as this gave him the morning to work on the house. It was not long before we had a comfortable home with a wood-burning stove in the living room, which warmed the whole house. We kept a pan on the stove all day for stews, hot water, etc.

Art started a huge garden, using his rototiller to clear the neglected flat area. I became mother to chickens, ducks, cats and a small dog named Pepe, whom we had rescued from a house which was being closed down and where we went to buy some antique furniture. The owner mentioned that he was taking Pepe to be 'put down,' as he was an older dog and he himself was moving into a retirement home. Art and I looked at each other and together said, "We'll take him with the furniture." Pepe, we discovered, was female; she lived eight more years with us.

On our first trip down into the town of Gold Beach we found the Catholic Church, a small building with a prominent board outside which we went up to read. Mass was on Sunday at nine a.m. As we turned away we were approached by a small priest, Fr. Joseph Black, who introduced himself and welcomed us to the area and to the church. He was a fine fellow of Irish descent.

"The church is served from Brookings which is thirty miles up the road. I am here every Sunday, but not usually during the week; there is no rectory. We only have about seventy-five families," he explained. We chatted for a while, and then told him we would see him at church. He replied, "See you on Sunday!" and was gone.

After some months of meeting parishioners at Sunday Mass, many of us would take Fr. Black to breakfast. There, we discussed the possibility of building a room at the rear of the church so that we could have a resident pastor. Several parishioners were contractors, and as there was already a shower and restroom in the sacristy, the men agreed to work on this project. Many other parishioners who had restaurants and hotels offered to assist.

The retirement home for priests in Portland sent us an active seventy-five year old Jesuit who would live in our building. As he had been teaching in seminary all his life, he never learned to drive nor had he ever cooked a meal. We parishioners had the answer; we bought him a microwave oven and an electric kettle. We discovered that Fr. Wolf was a great walker. We often met him on his way home from the shops and would give him a lift. Other days, various parishioners invited him to their homes. We know he enjoyed his time in Gold Beach. He stayed with us for five years, until his health deteriorated, causing him to return to Portland. Another retired priest soon replaced our Jesuit friend as pastor.

Brookings, the nearest town on the coast, ran a weekly newspaper. One day an advertisement read, "We're looking for a stringer to write a social column each week." I applied. The column was headed ROGUISH EYES. I was offered the job. It required me keeping my eyes and ears open for tidbits of current social interest. It mentioned birthdays, trips, and celebrations of many kinds, and named many people who were involved. I remember the Oregon Jazz Band, led by Bill Borcher, that came to town and gave us an outstanding performance. The Soroptimists and the Rotary Club always had something interesting going on. Valentine's Day and Christmas seem to be the most popular time for celebrations, but in this small city there was always something going on. I spent a great deal of time on the phone interviewing people for my column; it was fun.

At the small Curry County hospital, I studied for a Certified Nurse's certificate.

Later, Art and I both took Emergency Medical Training. The Fire Department and ambulance service in our area was run mostly by volunteers.

Letitia was one of the friends whom we made through church. On Sundays after Mass, we would all go out to breakfast, taking our pastor with us. She was also the head social worker in Gold Beach.

"We could really use you two as foster parents, we are so short of good homes," she told us over breakfast one Sunday. We subsequently fostered two seventeen year-old boys until they left the jurisdiction of the Children's Department. We had no children of our own and it was considered that these young men would relate better to adults.

At first, the boys we fostered behaved quite well, but it was not long before we had phone calls from the authorities that one or both boys had been detained for one or several incidents. We would then go and bail them out of jail. One day, I caught one of the lads running down the garden, carrying the bedspread off our bed filled with all kinds of valuables from our house. He was persuaded to come back, this time without police involvement.

We found them jobs at the fish cannery working weekend nights, hoping this would deter their mischief during the day. At last the day arrived when they turned eighteen. One boy went off to live with a grandparent; the other joined the army.

Later, our house became the emergency shelter for children needing immediate help. Sometimes the parents had been arrested or were in an accident. Usually after a few days the situation was resolved; either the parents returned, or a relative was found to take the little ones. The youngsters often arrived at night, accompanied by a policewoman. We kept beds made up. They were always terribly frightened; kindness and hot chocolate usually settled them down.

We had children of all ages, sometimes four or five siblings at one time. We watched as the elder ones took care of the younger ones. They enjoyed playing the piano, collecting the chicken and duck eggs or just following us around, helping me cook and make beds. Eventually the city opened a 'home' for children and we were no longer needed in that capacity.

Once more Letitia, our friendly social worker, knocked on our door, asking us if we could consider giving a home to an elderly lady who could no longer manage on her own.

Before many weeks passed we had two old ladies, one in her ninety-fifth year. The other had suffered a stroke and used a walker. Then came the father of a friend who needed a little help and companionship during the week when his daughter was working. Art redesigned the garage and made another large bedroom and bathroom which the elderly gentlemen moved into.

Mary, the older lady, was legally blind. However, she was able to dress herself. Her day started early; wearing an apron, she would wait for me to set up a card table with various beads in separate jars, whereupon she would commence to make beautiful necklaces. She worked for hours, feeling her way from one color to the next, involving several rows of different sized beads. The end result was a colorful lacey necklace to which I then fixed a hook to fasten it. Mary was a dear person- the only time I saw her annoyed was when she ran out of thread and had to wait for someone to refill her needle.

"Mary, do you have any grandchildren?" I asked her one day.

"Well yes, I have a grandson, Mark; he'd be about twenty. He's my son's boy. I don't know where he is now."

I was curious because Mary had the same last name as one of our foster boys. Later, I found out that indeed we had Mark's grandmother with us, using his old bedroom.

Both Tom's wife, Ellen, and brother, Dick, passed away while we lived in Oregon. Tom came to live in one of our apartments; he needed to be cared for and I looked after him, taking him his meals and keeping the place clean. He was not an easy man to care for. After about eighteen months, he too passed away.

One of Art's hobbies was engraving. He had learned this skill while working for a jeweler in Palo Alto during school summer vacation. We noticed that the schools, churches, and sport clubs had to travel to Portland, Eugene, or Medford to get work done on their trophies and plaques. Art set up his machine and started engraving everything the town needed; this was done in the mornings before he went to the mill. We quickly learned that people in the country liked to pay for their goods in kind. Our freezer was soon loaded with salmon, crab, venison, and even bear meat.

One day at the supermarket I met Mary and Brad. She was English and we became good friends. She was from Oxfordshire in England, the daughter of a clergyman in a country church. Brad was different; he had made his home in many parts of America, making a living where and when he could. He was primarily an artist. He'd built a rough cabin high in the hill behind Gold Beach on a large piece of land; Mary and Brad made their home there.

As money was always short, Brad had painted several large playing cards on the wood floor in lieu of rugs. Mary now had a little home she was proud of, a garden to grow produce, chickens, and a goat. Her mentor and neighbor, a kind elderly farmer's wife, taught Mary how to ride a horse, and then took her out one day with her shotgun. They were going to hunt for deer. Instead, they came upon a black bear. Quickly and quietly she gave Mary the shotgun, whispering, "You're closer to it; now aim carefully and just pull the trigger."

Mary came home proudly bearing the carcass of the bear across her saddle. She got her deer the following week.

When Mary's parents announced they were coming for a visit, we considered the culture shock they would receive. It was with great tribulation that Brad, who incidentally cleaned up for the occasion (Mary having cut his unruly hair), went to meet the minister and his lady at the airport in Eugene, three hours' drive from Gold Beach.

Art and I visited the family in their cabin a few days later, wondering what we would find. "Maybe they already have taken their daughter back to England," I ventured to Art.

We found Mary's father, the clergyman, building a chicken coop, hammering away happily. Upon entering the cabin, we found Mary's mother- a tall slim stately lady with grey hair fixed in a bun- wearing white gloves. She was preparing a large quantity of green beans for the freezer, humming as she worked. They seemed to have accepted the change in lifestyle quite smoothly.

Mary and Brad had a son and for some time all went well. Brad used his artistic skills to make a living in town painting, building and doing remodeling jobs. We lost touch with them after we left Oregon.

Some years later, however, we were traveling through Oxfordshire and remembered the little village Mary had come from. We found the church and knocked on the rectory door. Mary's mother greeted us warmly. Inside, we found Mary and the little boy. She had not been long home. We did not ask questions, but gathered that things had not worked out. Brad had disappeared, leaving Mary alone with the baby. She seemed to have mixed emotions, but was truly happy to be home. The parents were obviously delighted with their grandchild.

RETURN TO CALIFORNIA

When Art's mother passed away, I offered to write letters to all her friends and acquaintances. One of these was an eighty- year-old lady named Margo Bandini who lived in Fallbrook, California. It happened that she was a distant relative, her husband being a cousin of Art's father. Art remembered meeting her once, as a teenager, when she visited their home, but I had never even heard of her; she was about to change my life.

As a result of my letter to Margo, we started up a correspondence, in which she urged us- if we ever thought of moving- to consider going south to her part of southern California. Some months later we took a long trip down to Fallbrook, and after spending a week looking around Oceanside, Escondido, Vista, and Fallbrook, we eventually decided to leave Gold Beach and make this area our next home. We needed a change of lifestyle, and we had become really tired of the amount of rain we had each year in Oregon. There were several concerns that had grown as the years had gone by.

The economic situation, regarding the lumber business, was becoming worrisome. How many more trees could be cut down without ruining the environment, and more pertinent to us, how much longer could the mill stay open? Fewer areas were available for logging. Large Japanese vessels would come into Coos Bay

Harbor nearby, take all the sawdust and wood chips they could get, return to sea, whereupon they would turn the chips into particle board onboard ship, returning to the shore to sell their product in America.

The fishing industry was declining. Disease was killing off the salmon. We went up the Rogue River by boat to Blossom Bar one day and were shocked by the number of dead salmon floating in the water. No one, it seemed, knew what to do about it.

Tourism and the lumber mill were the only means of support in Gold Beach. The tourist season lasted about three months: June, July and August. Then came the dry months; the area became depressed and the rains came. We started to daydream of hot sunny days in southern California.

Another concern was that the state of Oregon built two blocks of subsidized apartments, right on our beach, with wonderful views. It became evident that no one would want to live in our older apartments. The two ladies we cared for moved to other facilities.

We decided it was time to consider moving back to California. After living in this idyllic spot for six years, we learned that you could not live on beauty alone. Driving home to Oregon we happily planned our future strategy.

Our house in Oregon went on the market; it didn't take long to sell. Soon we loaded up the U-Haul, collected our two Burmese cats and Pepe, always happy to go places, and off we drove down south. The cats decided to lie on the dashboard of the van in the sun the whole way down.

Margo Bandini was a generous lady; she calmly took us all in. Pepe was given a rustic abode in the woodshed with a long rope enabling her to investigate the garden; the cats were taken to a pet hotel in town. We cooked for Margo and looked after ourselves.

A large rambler-type house came on the market, situated in a quiet cul-de-sac on an acre of land. It had several bedrooms all on one floor. Art and I decided we would set up a Board and Care Home for the elderly and we applied for a license. This took some time. We were visited by an official of the welfare department in San Diego, who scrutinized our home, measuring bedroom sizes; each room had to be a minimum of 144 square feet. Then, I was asked to produce complete daily menus for two weeks. It was also necessary to have a list of occupational therapy that would be available for the clients. Everything was inspected thoroughly; the house was made ready to receive five or six elderly ambulatory folks.

Art worked on the large garden, which had three sides, the back leading into an avocado orchard. He planted many fruit trees, but made sure there were plenty of flowers growing outside the client's rooms. He also set up an engraving shop in our garage. There were no other engravers in the area; people took their work to San Diego or Escondido, thirty to forty miles away. Soon, he became very busy making plaques, engraving trophies for golf clubs, little leagues, all the schools, sports clubs, and churches.

An advertisement for the Board and Care Home in the local paper brought good results. In a couple of weeks, we were full. With the exception of a married couple, who had the master suite, they all had their own rooms with sliding glass doors leading out to the garden.

As well as cooking, I would drive the clients to the hairdresser or the doctor's office, then do the shopping, collecting them later. I enjoyed our busy life.

Margo came over very frequently. She would sit on a stool in the kitchen and watch me as I prepared the meals. Sipping a glass of wine, she would keep me company. As she was in her eighties then, we thought that we might need to give her a home later on. This was not her plan, however, and even when she broke her hip and spent time in the hospital, she returned to her own home with home care assistance, living there for another ten years.

We all ate together in the dining room. Although we had a sitting room for the clients we discovered that it was simpler for each client to have his own television. It didn't take long to see that some people had to have the volume up high, while others wanted a different program, or needed to sit close up to the set.

One man, Ed, was legally blind. He needed his reading book cassette to be set up in his room, whereupon he would listen for a few minutes, then fall asleep, missing pages of the story as the tape ran on. He was not a happy man; his two sons visited once in a while. They would creep into his room, see that he was asleep, and hurry out again. I would always insist that they go back and wake him up. "You're dad has been longing to see you; he will be so upset if he didn't get to have a chat with you," I would say.

Louisa, one of our ladies, ordered the Los Angeles Times to be delivered. After breakfast, she would don a plastic apron to prevent the print from getting on her clothes. Then she would sit down and read the paper cover to cover.

We took in another man who could no longer stay with his brother nearby. When he and Louisa met, they soon realized that they had been at school together in Durango, Colorado, fifty years before.

It was extremely difficult to get any reliable domestic help. They spoke little or no English; I had help with cleaning the house and bathing the clients, but as everyone needed pills at different times or were on a diet of some kind, I found it increasingly difficult to take time off. I worked a seven day week, which mostly I enjoyed. However, after three years, I got an ulcer. By this time, Art had moved his engraving business into a shop in Fallbrook, and was doing well. This left me alone with the patients most of the time.

We decided to put the house on the market as a Board and Care Home. A doctor's widow bought it, bringing with her some members of her family to help. All the patients were able to stay, and we moved out, continuing to take responsibility for everything for about six months, until the new owner was able to get a license.

SOMETHING NEW FOR US

Art decided that he wanted to become a real estate agent. He studied in the evenings, and once he had his license, he talked to a commercial realtor who found him a buyer for the engraving business, which he sold for a good profit. Meanwhile, we had moved temporarily into a mobile home, while we decided where we would next make our mark on the world.

Everyone was doing it- it seemed the thing to do.

"How do I learn the computer?" I asked a school counselor.

"California has a Regional Occupational Program, which is a government sponsored help program, for people wanting to get back into the workplace. You would be eligible for that."

I took classes in computer studies mornings, afternoons and evenings, at Vista high school. It felt strange being with young people all the time, but we all helped each other through difficult lessons. There was a different teacher in the evenings from the one during the day. This helped me, as one teacher would explain things in a way that I might not have understood from the other. After being away from formal learning for so many years, it wasn't easy to retain knowledge.

Overall, it was enjoyable. I felt a sense of accomplishment, being able to learn a new science.

Most days Art and I drove by an interesting red brick building in Oceanside. "What is that place?" I asked him.

"That's the Blade Tribune- you know, the newspaper office."

"I'd like to work there. I wonder if I could get an application form."

And so, my life turned about once more. I went to work in advertising, starting work at eight a.m.

At work in Oceanside at the Blade

LIFE IN OCEANSIDE, 1984-1999

This beautiful city on the west coast of America is just 45 miles from San Diego. Oceanside is next to the Marine base of Camp Pendleton, which has hundreds of miles of coast and inland rolling hills; training ground for the troops. The daily newspaper I worked on also published a weekly paper for Camp Pendleton and even one for the navy in San Diego.

Art and I found our house very quickly. It was just two blocks from the newspaper office so I was able to walk to work. At lunchtime, I took my lunch two more blocks to the beach and sat enjoying the sea breezes. It was an idyllic life. Meanwhile, Art enjoyed his new life selling houses. He worked hard on our garden growing oranges, avocados, figs and even bananas. He grew most of our vegetables. I started a collection of orchids. He built a patio out the back, a perfect addition for this area. The climate in Oceanside was never too hot or too cold, being on the coast.

Many interesting events occurred while I was at my desk. One day an elderly lady, tall and slim dressed all in black, approached me and asked if I could help her find somewhere to live for the next four months. Her appearance reminded me of Mary Poppins. She told me she had come over from England for the winter and that she didn't like the cold. She added she would cook a meal for a family or look after children; a room was all she needed. It was lunchtime, and Art was to pick me up. I asked her to wait so that I could introduce her to my husband. We took her home to lunch, showed her a spare bedroom and she moved in with us.

A delightful single lady; every day she took the bus or train and traveled all over the area, getting back in time for dinner. We enjoyed her company, especially hearing about her exciting days out, where she went and who she met. In due course she left, returning to her home in southern England. We visited her some years later. By then she was almost blind and walked with a cane, but obviously loved showing us around her little world.

On another day, an older man came up to my desk.. He had a strong northern English accent. I don't remember what he advertised but we starting talking. I learned he had worked in the coal mine all during WWII and after, until he came to America via Canada with his wife of many years.

Something made me ask him, "Do you get your pension from England?"

"Oh no," he replied. "We've left there now." I told him he would be eligible, and as I had an application form I could let him have, suggested he return for it the next day. This he did.

Months went by; then one morning I was busy working when a fifty dollar bill came fluttering on to my desk. Looking up, I saw our friendly miner with a grin on his face. He told me that he had applied for his pension and had received all the back pay owed to him.

"And what is more," he exclaimed, "My wife has got her pension too, and this is for you." He indicated the fifty dollar bill.

I told him how happy I was for him, but that I could not accept his gift or I would lose my job. He understood.

Another day a young Middle Eastern woman came by to advertise rooms for rent. She came by several times after that we spoke. Later, she came by to say she would not be around for six months. I asked why.

"I'm going to jail," she informed me.

Months later, she came by my desk again. I asked her, "How was it?"

"Oh, it was great!" She laughed. "I got to swim every day and I've lost weight. It wasn't bad at all."

SOPHIE THE PILOT

Art decided to join the Chamber of Commerce to help him with his real estate business. One evening the Chamber had a 'sundowner' at the flying club where we met John, who worked at the airport. He told us there was a young lady coming to learn to fly from Brest, France. She would be here for three months and needed somewhere to stay. We told him we will be happy to have her room with us.

Sophie arrived the following week. The airport had arranged a hire car for her, which she now unloaded, bringing cases and packages into the house.

I watched my husband's eyes sparkle. This girl was a beauty, tall and elegantly slim, her long dark hair coiled into a corkscrew over her right shoulder. Her tight plum colored pants creased as she bent to pick up her case. Art hurried to assist her.

She spoke in broken English. "I'm sorry, my Eengleesh is forgotten. It is so bad."

"Don't worry," I reassured her, "I speak a little French. Between us we will manage well."

After she had settled in, I gave her a door key, saying, "One thing we do not want is you having people stay the night."

"Oh la la, me? I'm a married lady!" She was quite shocked that I should mention this.

Sophie became part of our family immediately, offering to help in the kitchen, or to set the table for dinner. Her English improved within a week. She told us she had been in America before, reading a paper concerning her PhD in Oceanography. The laboratory where she worked in Brest, France had given her time off to come over to America to learn to fly.

"You see, it is less expensive to learn to fly here. The price of fuel is one quarter what it is in my country," she explained. "Also, where I live it is always very windy; Brest is on the peninsula that juts out just below England- here, I show you on a map. It is difficult to fly out of there."

Our new French friend was to find out that California weather can be unpredictable. Many days she would come home disappointed. "No flying today. Too much low cloud" or "It rained again. My instructor Ted will not let me fly when it rains."

She studied continuously, sometimes late into the evening. Her dictionary was always with her.

"It must be difficult for Sophie to learn everything in English," I commented to Art. "When she returns to France, she will have to re-learn everything in French."

One day Sophie came home full of excitement. "I flew by myself! I did the 'touch and go's' all by myself. Now I must go and e-mail Christopher and let him know what a clever wife he has," she laughed.

Art let her use our computer. Each day there was a letter from Christopher, who planned on coming over for two weeks once Sophie had her license. They planned on taking a trip around southern California.

Gradually the written tests were passed, then came the day for her cross country run. Almost three hours, in her own plane, being instructed as she traveled to take a certain route, then to change plans and re-route to a different height and speed. She had to calculate the time it would take, how much fuel she would use, etc and report this back to her ground contact, an examiner she had never met. Once again she came home to us radiant, having passed this test.

Ted, her instructor, called in the afternoon. "I know it's raining Sophie, but I'll go up with you this evening. We'll do some instrument flying."

Some hours passed. Sophie arrived home in tears, terribly upset.

"Whatever happened?" I asked.

"Oh, mon Dieu, I passed out on the plane! I don't know why- all I remember was Ted shaking me, saying 'I have emergency crews standing by; we're landing immediately.'"

The paramedics talked to Sophie, then took her to the Emergency department of the hospital. She was examined thoroughly, but nothing wrong could be found. She was advised to go to the airport doctor, which she did the next day. He found her physically sound as well. However, he refused to give her permission to fly in this country.

I sympathized with her. "Poor Sophie, what a terrible disappointment for you! What will you do now?"

"I will telephone Christopher; perhaps he can come over now. May he stay here with me if he comes?"

"Of course, may dear. You can get started on your trip once he has recovered from the plane journey."

Christopher came in a couple of days. They left for Palm Springs, the Grand Canyon, and Las Vegas, returning to us for one night. It was hard to say 'au revoir' to our beautiful French friend.

When I went into Sophie's room to clear up, I found a parcel addressed to me. It was from Sophie's parents, a thank you for looking after her. It was a beautiful book on France.

We have heard from Sophie by e-mail since her return to France. Her doctor determined the cause of her losing consciousness as being most probably dehydration. She remembered she had very little to eat or drink on that fateful day.

"Thank goodness she had her instructor with her," I commented to Art as we remade the bed.

Veronica and Sophie

THE SECOND PILOT

"Hi Veronica, this is John from the airport. How would you like to have another student pilot stay with you? This is a young man, and it would be for about seven or eight weeks."

"Well, I suppose I could; we certainly enjoyed having Sophie stay with us. Tell me when he will come."

"I'm picking him up tomorrow from San Diego. His name is Robert, and he comes from Surrey, England. He came over earlier this year on holiday with his father and they made enquiries about flying lessons. His plane arrives about two, so I expect we'll be there about four p.m."

"O.K. John, thanks. I'll see you then."

Next day, John arrived, accompanied by a fair-haired smiling young man, carrying only a golf bag.

"Hello, I'm Robert. They're sending my big case down later; it's lost." He sounded weary and a little resigned.

I showed him his room and went off to make tea. After this, John left, saying there was a car waiting for Robert in San Diego, and tomorrow we could put him on the train to go collect it.

After a while Robert came into the kitchen, looking around shyly. "Are there any pubs near here?" he asked.

"There are some bars not far away, but they are not the same as in England." I did my best to explain the difference.

"Well, where can I get some beer?" I pointed him in the direction of the Seven Eleven down the road. "I'll be right back," he called as he hurried out of the house.

Soon my husband came home.

"Oh Art, honey," I greeted him, and then explained the situation. "The boy has arrived from England and he's already out buying beer."

"He's just missing his buddies and probably tired after that long flight. After all, he's going to be taking flying lessons all the time and studying aeronautics; he'll have to keep a clear head. Don't worry- offer him some dinner and let him get some rest."

Next day, when Robert had gone off to collect his car, I sneaked into his room. He'd only drunk part of one beer out of the six pack; I was very relieved.

At first, it was like entertaining an alien from another planet. At age twenty-three, Robert had a very different view of life from us. He had obviously come from a wealthy family, judging by his belongings. His room smelled of leather- boots, jackets, toiletries in leather cases. The golf bag bore a well-known gold embossed name along the side. While most of his clothes were black, there were a couple white outfits which appeared later when he left to play a quick nine holes at the country club.

Once Monday morning came, he was up and at breakfast at eight o'clock, then down to the flying club for his first lesson. His instructor must have had a great pep talk with him; he applied himself well to studying, most of which he did at the airport.

"It's going to be more study than flying," Robert commented after his first day.

"Did you actually fly today?" I asked.

"Yes- well, at least Ted let me think I did. It was really terrific, either way."

He had so much energy. When he wasn't at the flying club, where he flew twice a day, he would run home, collect his golf gear and disappear for the rest of the daylight. At dusk he would return, have a shower and depart, wearing a trendy outfit, to find an interesting bar to eat in. He quickly found places with a television, showing sports. He settled in well.

We often asked him to eat with us at night, but he preferred to go 'downtown,' as he called it.

"It must be very hard to meet people here," I mentioned to Art. "No one goes dancing these days. The bars are about the only place I suppose- or the beach. Perhaps if Robert belonged to a church he'd meet people there, but he said he'd never subscribed to one!"

One night Robert did not come home. About ten o'clock the next morning he came in. "Hello, how's everything?" he called breezily from the kitchen.

I bit my tongue, then said, "All right, but what happened to you?"

"Oh, I met a girl."

That was all he would say. I rambled on about thinking he was in jail, or dead.

"I'm sorry, I should have phoned you. I'm fine. Got a flying lesson in half an hour, must hurry."

As the weeks passed we became closer to this young man. We didn't worry if he stayed out all night. He showed us in many ways he was a responsible adult: he never appeared to have had too much to drink but on several occasions his car was missing in the morning.

When we asked what happened, he replied, "Oh, I got a taxi home. You know the laws around here. May I use the phone? I need to get a taxi back to the Sandbar to pick up my car."

Robert is a pilot now, with an international license. He took his girlfriend out flying the day before he left. We never did meet her, but his bed was often not slept in.

CONCORDE

Art and I liked to go over to England every few years to see my family. We found a suitable time in the spring of 1995 and booked with British Airways .We were to leave Los Angeles in the late afternoon on a 747, direct to Gatwick.

At the airport we waited patiently, but our plane was delayed and delayed. Eventually we were told that our plane would not be coming; however, we would be taken to New York on another airline and then British Airways would get us to England.

It was close to nine p.m. when we boarded a B.E.A. plane. We had had no dinner but we hoped they would feed us. We had not been flying for more than an hour when I smelled smoke. We told the hostess, who went away towards the flight deck. Not many moments later the pilot announced that we would be making a stop in Las Vegas… "Your chance to have a little flutter," he commented. Later he spoke again. "If you happen to see any emergency vehicles, it's just normal procedure." Sure enough, there were several vehicles waiting as we landed in a far corner of the Las Vegas airport.

We were taken in to an empty hanger where we sat for some hours; eventually we all lay on the ground and tried to sleep. There were roughly ninety passengers. We were hungry and tired.

Eventually, we were told there was a plane waiting to take us to New York. We were served orange juice on board and for the next few hours we relaxed until dawn when the plane landed. As we left the plane, we were handed food coupons and shown the way to the cafeteria. We ate a hearty breakfast.

Some time later we were ushered into the Concorde waiting area where silver canisters of coffee tea and various tempting morsels were offered to us. I remember being asked if I would like to phone my family and being told, "Tell them you will be landing at Heathrow one hour earlier than you had planned."

We waited excitedly and watched as the big bird swaying slightly slid in close to our building. When she stopped, we marveled as the nose came up into flight position. The nose is lowered when she is on the ground to give better visibility. There are two complete and independent windshields. When the nose is raised, the plane has a complete aerodynamic shape. We were told our flight would take approximately three hours and twenty minutes. As we boarded we saw there were two seats each side of the isle. The plane seats 100 first class passengers. It appeared small compared to jumbo jets and DC10's. There was plenty of leg room, however.

We were informed we would be flying faster than a bullet, at twice the speed of sound. An elderly gentleman seated across the isle introduced me to his teenage granddaughter. He said he had flown Concorde innumerable times.

As we took off there was no unpleasant sensation, but a great force held us into the back of our seat. As the plane pressure stabilized at 6000 feet, we soon we saw a sign showing that we were at MACH I, the speed of sound. Later it reached MACH II, twice the speed of sound. We felt no movement as our plane reached its cruising speed at a height of 55,000 feet. The view from the window was magnificent; all around us was a perfect sunset, and looking up it was dark. What is seen as blue sky from the ground, we were told, astronauts see only black sky. This is due to the scattering of the earth's atmosphere, which is reduced the higher we travel. The only noise was the purr of the four Rolls Royce engines.

During our flight we were served a superb six-course meal on china plates with linen cloths. Our steward explained that all the food served had been flown in on a previous Concorde and prepared immediately. The meal started with caviar Strasburg foie grass, followed by prawn canapés, then prime rib and fresh vegetables. Next came a selection of cheeses, followed by strawberries Romanoff topped with double cream. Of course, the meal was accompanied with appropriate wines. As we finished our coffee, we were aware that we were descending. Our landing was smooth. Our journey from New York to London took three hours and two minutes. Concorde's fastest time was two hours and 57 minutes.

During the flight, we were allowed to visit the cockpit and were introduced to the pilot, co-pilot and flight engineer. We were awed by the amount of gauges and meters covering floor to ceiling. The pilot explained that the plane would be landed completely by the ground staff at London airport. Concorde is only permitted to fly supersonic over water, which is why it had limited use.

Concorde is no longer flying.

Concorde Jet
-British Airways

MOVE TO WASHINGTON
APRIL 1999

We enjoyed twenty years working in California, but when Art retired from Real Estate we decided to move once more. Several of our vacations had taken us up to Canada through the Puget Sound area; Art loved the mountains and the cool climate. He often mentioned that we should retire to a cooler, quieter area.

"After all," he would say, "When we first moved to Oceanside the population was 75 thousand; now it is 175 thousand." All the hills around us that had been golden (I had thought they grew wheat; it was scorched grass) were now covered in wood and cement buildings. We saw houses everywhere, cascading down the hillsides. The roads were mostly the same, but with each house having say, two cars, the traffic jams became tremendous.

We came up to Washington to meet my brother Ken and his wife Pat who were traveling from England. We met in Seattle and toured the area with them. Port Angeles, with its excellent college tucked in the tall trees and first class hospital would be good assets, plus the lengthy and beautiful waterfront. The Olympic Mountains behind us were majestic snow-covered temples of tranquility. Our decision was made; we loved the area. My brother went home and we decided to make one more move.

Our house in Oceanside sold quickly, giving us capital for the future.

Once we arrived in Port Angeles, we took a rental and looked around the area. We wanted a fairly big house. Although there were only the two of us, we always seemed to have people staying. At the top of a hill on the west side of town, one mile up from the Strait of Juan de Fuca and near the Catholic Church, we found our new home. The view from the living room gave us a ninety-degree view of the water. We could watch the ferry coming in and see the white caps if the water was rough. Sometimes cruise ships went by, looking elegant all lit up at night.

No sooner had we settled in and joined the Newcomers Club, we went up to the beautiful Peninsula College to sign on for some courses. Then we joined a hiking group and of course became acquainted with Queen of Angels Catholic Church community. Our lives were busy; Art worked on the large garden which was on a hill. He built a ten-by-twenty-foot pond with a waterfall. In our neighborhood, people offered us fish for the pond and plants for the garden. To our delight we had found ourselves in a friendly, warm neighborhood.

How could we have guessed yet another exciting chapter of our lives lay ahead.

CHINA EXCHANGE

It was not until late in September 2000 that I had considered China in any depth; it was just one of those countries in Asia along with Japan, Indonesia etc. Art and I were attending the local college for computer classes. Some of the lunch hour presentations in the 'Little Theater' of the college were interesting, and on this day there was to be a session on China. I decided to go; Art was still in his class.

As, usual, the theater was full. What I saw and heard during the following hour changed the path of my life.

I learned that there was a contract signed between one of the universities in China and our college for one year and for that reason some personnel from Guilin University, of Guanxci province had come over to be part of the program. First, a professor from our college who had been in Guilin for a semester showed slides of the campus and talked about his life in the huge school of 14,000 students and 300 faculty (fifty of which were teachers in English). He showed slides of his apartment and some of the classrooms, dormitories, etc. This campus covered many acres and was surrounded by lawns and lovely landscaping. No building was constructed over six stories and there was a unanimity in that they all had bright blue roofs and white cement walls.

After this, a Chinese professor who had been teaching Chinese at our college for some months gave a comparison of his life here with that in Guilin.

Finally, one of the visiting Chinese men spoke about the need for adults to go to China and teach oral English at their university. They would have an apartment on campus like all the other teachers. They would be paid and would be well looked after by the office of International Cooperation at the university, which was working with the office here in Port Angeles, Washington.

I was fascinated. I remembered that I had a certificate to teach English as a second language filed away in a drawer. After the presentation was over I went up and talked to one of the visiting gentlemen who spoke excellent English. Having explained that I was interested and that I had a suitable qualification, I felt the excitement between us grow. I added, "I have a husband."

"Bring him, bring him," he replied. "We need him."

At home, I relayed my interesting morning to Art, who laughed at my enthusiasm and mentioned a few realistic problems concerning leaving our house, the cats, etc. I thought, 'I might have known Art wouldn't be interested. It's too adventurous for him.' I dropped the matter.

Some days later, an excited husband came home from college. "Well, I think we might have solved the house sitting problem about going to China." I listened, amazed. "A girl in my class says she would like to stay here and mind our cats. She even offered to mow the lawns. You see, she lives outside Port Angeles and as we are so close to the college, it would save her money and she could even ride her bike to school."

And so that is how we started preparing to make a temporary yet radical change in the path of our lives. We were going to England for Christmas in a few weeks. In the meantime I joined the Chinese class to learn what I could about the country and its language and culture. The more I leaned, the more I was excited about the opportunity to see another part of the world and to learn about the Chinese people.

Our Christmas in England was slightly marred by the fact that our family thought we were crazy. Some even told us so; others were polite, asking us innumerable questions that we were unable to answer.

Once back in Washington, we sent off for our visas, had medical examinations and got hepatitis shots. Our flight was booked through Asiana Airlines. Our house sitter moved in as we left in mid February. We really had little information about where we were going. We had been warned that it would get very hot in Guilin so we left warm clothes behind. This was a terrible mistake because when we arrived the weather was cold; we froze.

Our unheated apartment- grand by Chinese standards- was equipped with minimal wooden furniture. The floors were tiled which made it seem colder. We had two bedrooms, a little living room complete with computer and e-mail so that we could 'keep in touch with our families' and a small kitchen with a gas tank for the two burner stove and to heat water for the shower.

Beyond the kitchen was our bathroom. I breathed a sigh of relief as I saw we had a Western toilet and a small washbasin. Most places had only a hole in the ground with two carved footprints from which to balance and aim. Our showerhead was almost over the toilet, meaning you could sit and shower if you felt so inclined. However, the water from the shower fell all over the tiled floor, which proved to be a slippery problem. There was a drain in the center of the room; we just had to mop up to dry the floor.

The walls were whitewashed and there were no carpets. The one twin sofa in the living room was wooden. There was a round table with one chair in front of the computer. Each bedroom had one single bed with sheets and a pillow, a duvet and a thin blanket the consistency of our towels.

We discovered a washing machine in the kitchen, the pipe from which would not extend to the sink, so the water from it had to go over the bathroom floor to the drain there, making it the cleanest floor in the apartment. The only hot water went into the shower.

We seldom cooked a meal, as there was an enormous cafeteria on campus about seven minutes' walk from where we lived. Due to the fact that several ethnic groups were studying at the university, there were many separate booths supplying hot meals of various types to suit the varied customs and cultures present.

We learned we should take our own bowl to the cafeteria, into which was first placed a spoonful of white sticky rice. Over this we then added any of several types of casserole, such as green bean and tofu, or pork pieces with carrots or other vegetables. There was chicken cut up into one-inch squares (including bones) in gravy with optional hot peppers. There was an infinite variety of dishes.

Art loved Guilin noodles for breakfast. These were rice noodles in a soup onto which could be added various flavorings and herbs. I found packets of cereal at a local store, to which I added hot water.

After a few days we were approached by the English Department head and many of his colleagues, who formally welcomed us to the campus. We were given our teaching assignments. We worked fifteen hours a week: some days, morning and afternoon or evening, but no Sundays. We actually had two days off a week in addition to Sunday.

This schedule allowed us to take the bus into Guilin town to shop and sightsee. It is a beautiful city surrounded by unusual hillskarsks as they are called- with sharp peaks of limestone. A huge building program was in progress while we were there, so there was dust, mud, and building materials all over the place. It seems when the government gives areas money to update the town, they start on the roads and buildings (pulling down old shacks) all at the same time. Our university had four new buildings being constructed at the time we were there; the scaffolding was all bamboo. Not much mechanical equipment is used, but hundreds of workers, including women, could be seen high up, standing and working in all weathers. This went on most of the day and night, seven days a week.

The campus was very large, with nicely landscaped areas around the various buildings. There was a spectacular library, gymnasium and students' hall. Sports facilities abounded.

Many of the students and faculty used bikes, most very old with metal seats for a passenger. The passengers would sit side-saddle on the back of the bike with their hands in their laps as they bumped over the uneven roads. A few of the teachers had motorcycles; not a single student had a car. In fact, on the streets most of the cars were old taxis or lorries carrying building supplies.

The streets were full of bikes and pedestrians, weaving their way through the open air markets that seemed to be there from early morning until late in the night, their stalls being lit by candles.

We were amazed at how young the students appeared. They were between twenty to twenty-four years of age, but many looked about ten. But it was their personalities that we grew to love. They have a simple, straightforward way about them. They could not do enough for us; if we wanted to go to town, they offered to accompany us so they could bargain for us. One day I had a sore throat, and after class some students walked me to a drug store, of which there were two kinds (one with a red cross, denoting prescriptions being sold there, the other with a green cross, meaning over the counter goods and cosmetics were sold there). They explained that I needed something for a sore throat and I was given a remedy. The students wanted to walk with you anywhere- to class, to your apartment- just so that they could speak English.

The girls were so feminine. Not many wore trousers. Their hair was usually short and straight, with no make-up or jewelry, only nail polish (which they loved). All the students were so considerate of older people- such as ourselves- rushing to help us at all times.

We did a lot of miming in the shops. In the bank, we would take a large bill and go as if to tear it across. The girls would smile and immediately give us small change- not a word was spoken. In the post office, after each letter was stamped it was returned to us. On a table stood an old fashioned glue pot. We would then stick the envelope down and hand it back to be mailed; the envelopes here had no sticky surface on them.

Student in front of fountain, Guilin Univeristy

SEARCH FOR A CHURCH

Before leaving for China, I had contacted the Maryknoll Fathers headquarters in New York to ask about a Catholic church in Guilin. For many years, the church in China has been persecuted and sadly not many people have had the opportunity to learn about the Catholic faith. They gave me valuable information and on the first Sunday morning accompanied by two students I took the bus to the terminal in downtown Guilin. The students were just curious and helpful hearted. We came to a building with wrought iron gates in front. On the wall was a plaque that read, "Mass: Saturday 6 p.m. Sunday 11 a.m." written in English.

We went inside. It was like a big hall with a stage. Quite a few people sat inside, mostly families. Soon a woman came on to the platform and obviously started to teach the audience some songs in Chinese. This took about ½ hour. Then about 30 women dressed beautifully in flowing long silk gowns in pastel shades processed up the isle and began to sing. They sang in parts and sometimes the audience joined in. Then they left. This took about another ½ hour. Finally, yet another woman started reading (perhaps from a Bible) for a while. At this point we decided to leave. There was no sign of a priest, an altar or Mass preparation.

A few days later, Art and I were having lunch high up on the 6th floor of a store in the restaurant and out of the window we saw a church. One end had an onion dome, the other a steeple. We hurried to find this church. The door was open but when we tried to walk in we could not enter. The floor had been torn up and was covered in large rocks. Looking around we saw a man high up on a ladder working. He acknowledged us but as we had no Chinese we could not communicate. He continued working.

Some months later, Art went by again. He discovered there was to be a grand opening the next Sunday. He was able to go to Mass, all in Chinese, with about 65 other folks. At Christmas, the church was decorated. There was a beautiful crèche with the holy family.

謹賀新年

WISHING YOU A BRIGHT AND HAPPY HOLIDAY SEASON

SEASON'S GREETINGS AND BEST WISHES FOR THE NEW YEAR.

(Art returned to Guilin for another 6 months, after we came home to Washington State. He was able to attend Mass each week.)

Everything was so inexpensive. Art loved to get his hair (what there was left of it,) washed, as the girl would massage his scalp, shoulders, arms, to his fingertips, and down his back. When they start to wash your hair there, there is no water involved; they put shampoo on and work it in, then as the foam expands, they plop it into a basket and repeat several more times. Eventually they take you over to a basin a rinse your hair off. All this costs about five yuen, with eight yuen equaling one dollar. A meal in a restaurant for two costs about the same, and that would include several dishes.

Art and I each had a pair of shoes made by a little man in a shed-like shop just by the exit from our campus. He took cardboard and measured round our feet, took ten yuen and told us to come back in a week. We paid him another fifty yuen. It was under eight dollars for the shoes, which fit well and look smart.

There were many outings which we took in our spare time. There are eight parks in Guilin alone; all very beautiful, not full of flowers but attractive trees, foliage and lawns. The Li River runs through the city. Many tourists take a boat for the day and travel on the river which weaves around the stark-looking karsks for miles. Lunch is served on board; it is amazing what tasty food can be served with only the rear of the boat as the galley.

We took a bus to one of the beauty spots upriver called Yang Shuo. It took us an hour and cost us five yuen, but if we had gone by the faster tourist boat it would have been one hundred yuen. We saw fields of rice growing on our way there, being ploughed by water buffalo, which are as common as cows. Every blade of rice was planted by hand; there are no tractors. There were also groves of citrus trees. We were getting into warmer country as we went. We saw a man on a bike with a buffalo on a leash. Art saw a baby pig riding in the basket on the front of a bike.

Yang Shou is a tourist town with wonderful shops on the main west street, selling almost anything: silks, linens, china, pottery, fans, and jade. The menus in the restaurants were in English and Chinese. It had a holiday air about it- a fun place indeed.

One evening after class, we were asked by one of Art's classes to go to a restaurant in the market area. When we got there, all the students were in the back room, making jaoza (little tiny dumplings), which were then dumped into a big pot of boiling water. The water had to boil three times, we were told; each time a little cold water was added.

After they were cooked, the pastry was cut into circles and a little filling put in each. One filling was egg with green onion and herbs; another was a sausage mix. It was a great time. We were given tea, and there were little dishes of sauces you could dip your dumplings in. You were supposed to use chopsticks for this; the students were determined I should learn to use them, even left- handed, though this did faze them a bit.

There must have been twenty to twenty-five students there; most of the girls did the preparation. I helped for a while. The boys did some of the cooking.

I decided to go home after a couple of hours, while Art was going to stay and watch a badminton match. One of the boys came running after me. "I'll walk you home; the traffic [bikes] are bad at this time." I was touched by his thoughtfulness.

AN INCREDIBLE DAY OUT

One of the girl students asked if we would like to go to see the waterfalls, not too far away, she said. As we had Friday off, we agreed to go, and then remembered we had our Chinese painting class at 2:30 p.m.

"No problem," she said, "we can go and return by then." We arranged to meet her and some friends at 8 a.m. She told us to bring an umbrella as it might rain, and also some food, as there is nowhere near there to get any.

As usual, there was great confusion when we arrived; some boys had not arrived, so we waited. Then more discussion as to the route we should take. We thought they were going on the bus- in fact, three different buses- but then they decided we could take two of the little three-wheeled vehicles (like the Daf car), which is a glorified motor bike with an axle at the back and two wheels. The upper construction is metal bars with plywood attached and little windows, the top had a cover of sorts to keep the rain out.

The students haggled for ages and finally we were told, "You two go in this one, we five will take the other one."

There were just two seats in ours, linoleum covered. No springs, and of course no seat belts. (None are required in any vehicles, especially taxis). To get in was a task, as they are so small, with no head room. I found it awkward, but poor Art did have a struggle to get his long legs in. Anyway, we bounced our way along busy roads with food stalls each side, then into the country, with rice paddies all around.

At this point, the road wasn't covered and was full of potholes. We hung on, now and again almost turning over, as busses or lorries pushed us off a good part of the road. The top was so low that Art banged his head on several occasions. We passed a large prison with a high wall on top of which was a series of very lethal looking electric wires. There were guards at the corners, in high towers.

When we finally arrived at the resort, we saw some magnificent waterfalls, and took a long walk up steps and round a hillside. We went for a boat ride on a bamboo punt on a lake which was so serene and peaceful after our bumpy ride. A punt is made with strips of bamboo 8 feet long strung together with rope, making it buoyant but half submerged. The fishermen use these; standing in their punts, they have a long bamboo pole across their shoulders with a cormorant on each end. The birds dive and catch the fish, but are unable to consume them, as a tight string is tied round their necks. The fishermen are then able to take the fish from the bird.

There were loads of butterflies about too. Art spent time photographing baby water buffalo, working in the fields beside their mums. He also took lots of photos of the waterfalls. We had a great time with the students, who bartered for everything for us, and loved doing it! Eventually we had to leave and take our carriage back to the university.

We noticed old frail looking bridges in the countryside with delicate looking overgrown arches, looking like lace. Mostly women were working knee deep in the rice fields, thinning out the rice or planting the fine grassy strands. There were also many vegetable fields, some citrus groves- the road paralleled the beautiful Li Jiang River.

Next day Art and I took a walk past the cemetery which we could see from our apartment. This consists of many ten-foot diameter circles of rocks, four foot high with earth in the middle where flowers are grown. We wondered if families were buried standing up in these. During the time of Ching Ming (a time of remembrance for the dead), families visit the graves all together, taking with them colored paper marked with clothing, shoes, food etc… all of which is placed in the center of the circle and set on fire. The smoke from this symbolized the ascent of these goods for the use of the deceased. Then they would set off fire crackers.

Further on down the road were acres of tea plantations.

We took the bus into town from the campus one day and discovered the bus was full of small children colorfully dressed in party outfits. The bus was very full, with three children sitting on one seat. At a bus stop, an elderly lady got on to the bus and saw there were no seats. She simply picked up a small child on the end of a seat and sat down with the child on her lap. We all left the bus at a hotel where the children invited us in to watch them perform many dances and songs for us; it was Childrens' Day.

SUMMER STORM

I awoke one morning to the rumblings of thunder and the pounding of heavy rain. It wasn't cold, not even humid. It was time to get up anyway, as both Art and I had classes at 8:20 a.m. Looking out our open veranda I saw the piles of dumped red earth, which stretched the length of a football field. Today the valleys between the lumps looked like a network of lakes, some joining together to make the mounds look like islands. There was the typical wall surrounding our six blocks of teachers' living quarters, but the red lakes dribbled through and out on top the walking path where we would have to go to get to our classes.

By the time I had made some sloppy hot cereal, like semolina, for breakfast, the little gardens outside each building had disappeared under the red muddy wash. Happily I got out my yellow wellies bought in the outside market for eighteen yuen (around two dollars fifty cents); I could splash around in these and not get my feet wet. Art put on his hiking boots.

The thunder was noisier now but we had to get going. Once outside, we realized that the drains could not cope with the heavy rain and the red silt; by now washed-out weeds were finding their way to the drains. No one seemed to be doing anything about this mess, although our guard at his entry box shed kept up a friendly wave as everyone went by. I was scared—holding my umbrella with its metal frame in one hand and my school books in the other. We slipped around on the slimy ground, and I prayed I would not get hit by lightning. By the time we had progressed to the main road our buildings were on, we met up with throngs of students on bikes, spraying everyone as they wove their way through. There was construction of a new building in progress along this road, so even more rubble and stones were added to the mess. There were overloaded dump trucks carrying earth from the sites as well, dropping lumps of dirt and splashing everyone as they, the lords of the road, sped on.

Despite the noisy storm, we could see forty or more people high up on the bamboo scaffolding, continuing to work. There were no hard hats or yellow rain coats; just poor workers taking their chances high up on slim round bamboo poles, nailing and sawing pieces into place.

We said goodbye at the decorative fountain, which to my knowledge never performed, at the junction of two roads. Art went to Building No. Two, and I turned west and went to Building No. Six. Up on the second floor I squelched down the corridor, past the little spittoons outside every classroom door, until I breathed a sigh of relief and entered my class. The storm was almost over outside, but the windows had been left open and puddles of water were on the desks and floor. We used the far side of the room, leaving the now-bright sunshine to dry up the wet.

No student was missing from my class, but some shoes were left at the door to dry.

Art and I met at the fountain at noon. Most of the rain had evaporated, but the mud and slush still remained. We even saw a small fish trying to swim near one of the drains; we guessed he had come up earlier from the sewer. We saw him several days after, now dead and decomposing. Eventually he disappeared, hopefully being claimed as dinner by one of the few birds around.

The weather had gotten steadily warmer and by the end of May we were hot. We left on the 18th of June, and I am glad we did; the mosquitoes had found us, even though we slept under nets and there were screens in the windows. The classrooms had no air-conditioning, just two large fans in the front of the class. With all the construction outside, if we left the windows open the noise was bad, especially on days the lawnmowers were used.

China was an adventure and an experience that I would not have missed for the world. Our one thought has been that we were fortunate to meet the most beautiful people who enriched our lives. We hope that we have left behind us feelings of warm friendship, as we taught not just English but something of a way of life before unfamiliar to these people.

RETURN TO THE USA
JUNE 2001

The long journey home to Washington State via Tokyo was exciting, but we were happy to return home. The young girl who had looked after the house had done a good job and now left to return to her mother's house. After a few minutes of rejection, Buttons, our cat remembered us, greeting us warmly just as she did each time we went shopping.

We had been away for half a year; the experiences we had gained made our comfortable home more delightful with rich memories of that other world.

Art returned to China for another half year. Meanwhile I was asked by the college coordinator if I would like some company. He offered me two students from China who needed accommodation while they studied at the school.

Since that time we have enjoyed having students from Mongolia, Japan, and Kenya. Some students arrived with their parents who wanted to make sure their child would be in a safe environment. We housed the parents for a week, after which they returned home. We knew we had to have a large house when we arrived in Port Angeles and it has been put to good use. We have enjoyed meeting, feeding and reassuring those worried parents who left contentedly. The Chinese students particularly work hard; they are well disciplined and polite. We have learned much from our adventures up in Washington State and while we no longer travel to distant lands, we still have the opportunity to interact with different cultures through their people.

What a joy it had been to be useful, all the while collecting memories to laugh and sometimes cry over. God only knows what the future may bring. He has taken care of us thus far; we await His guidance once again.

Proceeds from this book will go to:
The Salesians of St. John Bosco and The Mary Knoll
Missions. Both work for children in 3rd world countries.